L.E.A.D.
OUT LOUD

Be Clear. Be Heard. Be Unstoppable.

ANTAWN KNIGHT

DEDICATION

To my family, my compass, my calm, my constant. You are woven into every chapter. Your love, laughter, and belief carried me through storms and stillness. If these words stand firm, it's because you've held me up repeatedly.

To the leaders rising now, whether you're stepping into your first challenge or scaling your next summit. This is your permission slip. Your battle cry. You don't need more credentials; you need clearer conviction. Legacy doesn't wait for a spotlight. It starts with your next step, even when your voice shakes.

Finally, to the quiet leaders, the ones lifting without applause, holding the line no one else sees, and moving mountains with silent conviction. This is your standing ovation. We see you and need you. Your presence is the pulse beneath true progress.

Keep pressing forward. Keep lifting others. Keep leading out loud.

If you let it, this journey won't just make you better. It will make you braver, and it will help someone else believe they can rise too.

CONTENTS

ACKNOWLEDGMENTS

No leader rises alone. This book is the result of a journey shaped by countless voices, challenges, lessons, and acts of support along the way.

To the Airmen, Soldiers, Sailors, Marines, Guardians, and civilian teammates I've had the honor of serving with, you've taught me what leadership looks like in real time: under pressure, in silence, through service, and in triumph. Thank you for inspiring me daily and reminding me that leadership begins with people.

To my mentors and peers, thank you for challenging my thinking, holding up the mirror, and urging me to grow. Your wisdom, honesty, and encouragement helped refine the voice behind this book.

To every student, workshop participant, and teammate who asked the hard questions, offered new perspectives, and listened with care, you've added fuel to this fire. Your stories helped shape mine.

To my family, thank you for being my constant. Your love, laughter, and sacrifices are stitched into every word on these pages. You've carried me when I needed it most.

To the future leaders, whether you're stepping into your first leadership role or evolving into your next one, this book is for you. May it remind you that your voice matters, your influence is real, and your legacy is being written every day.

And to those who lead quietly, courageously, and without recognition, this is your reminder that we see you and we need you. Keep leading out loud.

DISCLAIMER

The views and opinions expressed in this book are solely those of the author, Antawn Knight, and do not reflect the official policy or position of the United States Air Force, the Department of Defense, or any U.S. government agency. This work is the product of personal experience, research, and leadership insight, and is not endorsed by, or affiliated with, any military or governmental institution.

INTRODUCTION

This book was born from a truth I learned in the field, in the classroom, and in moments of crisis: leadership is not a title, it's a voice.

Leadership is the voice that calms a team during chaos. The voice that challenges without demeaning. The voice that says, "I believe in you," and means it. Leadership happens every time you speak up for what matters, lift others with clarity, or stand firm in your values.

In my over 15 years of military service, leading across continents, mentoring the next generation of leaders, and coordinating efforts among diverse agencies, I've seen firsthand the power of effective communication. I've also seen what happens when leaders go silent, lose clarity, or fail to connect with their teams.

L.E.A.D. Out Loud is my answer to that challenge. It's a guide, a call to action, and a toolkit all rolled into one. It's for the leaders who want to influence both outcomes and people. It is for those who want to lead with presence.

In this book, you'll find real stories, practical tools, and a model forged in the trenches of authentic leadership.

The L.E.A.D. Model is:

- Listen with intent
- Empower through communication

- **A**dapt and overcome
- **D**ecide and deliver

Whether you lead a squadron, a business, a classroom, or a community, this book is for you.

Because your leadership isn't just about what you do, it's about how you show up.

It's time to **Be Clear. Be Heard. Be Unstoppable.**

~ Antawn Knight

PART I

THE L.E.A.D. LEADERSHIP MODEL

Listen with intent

Empower through communication

Adapt and overcome

Decide and deliver

LISTEN WITH INTENT

> *"Most people do not listen with the intent to understand; they listen with the intent to reply."*
>
> ~ Stephen R. Covey

THE LEADERSHIP MISCONCEPTION

Early in my career, I really thought I had this leadership thing all figured out. I truly believed that leadership meant speaking up, having all the answers, and taking charge. I quickly learned that real leadership starts with listening.

I'm not talking about the act of simply hearing when someone talks and you are actively thinking or waiting for them to stop talking so you can utter out your response. I'm talking about truly listening, paying attention to what is being said, how it's being said, and perhaps most importantly, what is *not* being said.

During one of my deployment debriefs, I remember sitting across from an exhausted-looking Airman; his eyes were tired, and his posture was guarded. I'm sure the only thing keeping him up was caffeine and freedom. My first thought was to say something strong and motivational, but I didn't.

Instead, I asked him a question and then listened as he opened up to me. That moment taught me more than any textbook ever did; people are more likely to communicate when they feel heard. Leadership impact will always begin and end with listening.

🧠 WHAT IT MEANS TO LISTEN WITH INTENT

Listening with intent means being fully present and attentive. No phone and no half-nods. When you listen with intent, you are telling the other person:

- "You matter."
- "I'm with you."
- "I'm not waiting to speak; I'm here to understand."

If people don't feel heard, they won't hear you. Intentional listening comes first; only then do direction and correction stick."

🎧 LISTENING STYLES: PASSIVE VS. INTENTIONAL

Listening demands action, effort and intention. One small side thought during a conversation will leave you playing detective, trying to solve the mystery of the conversation.

Some people treat listening like a cheap umbrella in a windstorm; sure a few drops get through, but most of it slides right off. Others listen like its fresh rain after a long drought, every word lands, sinks and matters.

That level of intention separates passive listening from intentional listening. One style lets words pass by: the other lands and matters.

Passive Listening:

- Waiting for your turn to speak
- Jumping to conclusions
- Multitasking

Intentional Listening

- Asking clarifying questions
- Reflecting on what you heard
- Giving your full attention

☑ REAL-WORLD EXAMPLE: LISTENING BENEATH THE SURFACE

Years ago, I stepped into a leadership role where the mission was critical, and the stakes were extremely high. On the surface, the team appeared to be thriving, they were talented, motivated, capable, and were hitting all of their performance metrics.

Yet, something was off.

Beneath the surface, there was a lingering dissatisfaction. Communication was fragmented, and team members constantly came to me for answers while avoiding taking ownership of their own programs. Gossip was rife, and trust was low. As a result, morale was quietly eroding.

I could sense that the Airmen didn't feel heard, valued, or trusted.

So, I made a deliberate decision to begin listening with intent. I scheduled one-on-one sessions with every team member, reserving a full hour for each conversation. I even built in a 15-minute buffer between each meeting so I could be fully present.

I walked into each conversation with questions, instead of answers.

Questions such as:

"What would you change if you were in charge?"

"What's getting in the way of you owning this mission?"

When they answered, I didn't just nod, I empowered them. If they had a solution, I gave them the lead on implementing it.

We established daily, weekly, and monthly checkpoints to track progress and celebrate every achievement, regardless of its size.

Over time, trust replaced gossip and ownership replaced avoidance. That same team went on to deliver the most outstanding customer service support in the Air Force, and it all started with the decision to listen with intent.

📄 HISTORICAL EXAMPLE: ABRAHAM LINCOLN AND THE POWER OF LISTENING

During one of the most divided times in American history, President Abraham Lincoln led a fractured nation through the Civil War. During this crucial time, he led with both strategy and presence.

People knew Lincoln for walking the halls of the War Department, hospitals, and even receiving lines late into the night. He didn't go to lecture others, instead he went to listen.

He met with soldiers, generals, widows, and political rivals, not to defend his position, but to understand theirs.

He didn't interrupt and he didn't posture. Rather, he absorbed people's words, their fears, and their frustrations; even if he disagreed, people walked away believing they'd been heard by their President.

> *"I destroy my enemies when I make them my friends."*
>
> ~ Abraham Lincoln

In a time of national distrust, Lincoln's willingness to listen with empathy and patience became his greatest strength. His leadership didn't begin with answers. It began with understanding.

CONNECTION ACROSS TIME: LISTENING LEADERSHIP

It's remarkable to see the physical relief people experience when they feel genuinely heard; their shoulders ease, their guarded tone softens, and they start sharing ideas instead of objections, ultimately dropping the defensive posturing. You see glimpses of this thread throughout history. Abraham Lincoln didn't earn trust by bullying and intimidating critics; he built trust by listening to the fears of widows and the frustrations of generals, turning enemies into allies through understanding.

I've seen the same thing in offices and break rooms. When you honor someone's voice, you truly earn their belief in your leadership.

A team that felt overlooked will lean in when you sincerely ask for their perspective. You will also find people who once gossiped start bringing solutions, and even at home, listening without your phone can rebuild frayed bonds. You will be amazed to see the difference in morale and productivity that the power of listening can bring.

Listening is like opening a window on a stuffy day. It clears the air and gives everyone a chance to breathe, and one simple conversation can shift the course of a project or a life. The power of listening transcends across times and cultures, and the best leaders aren't the ones who shout the loudest but those who stand still long enough to hear the heartbeat of the people they serve.

🧠 LISTENING IN ACTION: LISTENING WITH INTENTIONAL IMPACT

Communication is the words you choose, but it's also how you frame your message, connect with your audience, and carry yourself in the moment. Clarity in communication comes when you:

- ☑ Think before you speak
- ☑ Speak with purpose
- ☑ Match tone to intent
- ☑ Cut clutter and highlight the core message
- ☑ Listen actively so your responses carry weight

"Leading without listening is like steering without a compass; you're moving, but you won't see the rocks until it's too late. The course of your leadership follows the course of your listening."

Listen to lead. The quality of your listening sets the quality of your leadership.

🛠 TOOLS FOR INTENTIONAL LISTENING

Let's say you have never used a wrench before, and your objective is to tighten a loose bolt. You identify which bolt you want to tighten to hold a door in place.

Your first step would be not just to clamp down and force a bolt into place, but you would need to feel for the threads, figure out which way the wrench needs to be turned, then turn slowly and gently, and tighten just enough to align everything.

Listening is like that. You get a feel for it, instead of grabbing at words, you can hear the pauses as well as the points, loosen up when there's strain, and focus when someone's meaning slips.

To practice listening, lean on these simple tools:

- **The 80/20 rule:** Listen 80% of the time, speak 20%.
- **3-Second pause:** Count to three before responding.
- **Paraphrase check:** *"So what I'm hearing is..."* confirms clarity.
- **Environmental control:** Put away the phone. Presence is power.

CHAPTER REFLECTION: LISTEN WITH INTENT

Listening isn't something you do out of politeness; it's a conscious choice to give someone your full attention. Think back to the last time you really tuned in, you put your phone down, stopped rehearsing your reply, and let the other person have the floor. That kind of listening takes discipline, curiosity, and humility; it's about making yourself small so someone else can be big. It is a sacred practice, when you treat listening as a strategy instead of a courtesy, it changes how people trust you and the quality of ideas I hear.

Ask yourself: am I listening to understand, or just rehearsing my response? When did someone last thank me for really hearing them out? How would my leadership look if listening sat at its center? What simple habits, pausing for a breath before I speak, reflecting back on what I heard, could help me make more space for other voices?

Reflection Questions:

- Do I listen to understand or to respond?
- When was the last time someone thanked me for listening to them?
- How would my leadership style change if I treated listening as a strategic action rather than just a courtesy??

💡 LEADERSHIP TOOL: LISTENING PREP & PRACTICE GUIDE

- ☑ Block 15 distraction-free minutes before your next one-on-one
- ☑ Prepare two open-ended questions
- ☑ Practice the 3-second pause in conversation
- ☑ Keep a weekly journal of listening breakthroughs

🧩 CONNECTION TO THE L.E.A.D. MODEL

Listening is the foundation of the L.E.A.D. Model. You can't empower, adapt, or deliver without first understanding. Listening centers your awareness and builds the trust that enables action.

Listen first. Lead forward.

🔊 LEADERSHIP BONUS NUGGET #1: LISTEN LOUDER THAN YOU LEAD

You Want to Lead For Real? Shut Up and Lean In.

MYTH: The best leaders command respect because their voice always fills the room. All eyes, all ears, all authority. You lead by making sure your point lands, first and last.

TRUTH: Want to know the leaders I remember? The ones whose impact actually shaped me. Not the talkers. The listeners. Anyone can fill the air with answers.

Few people make space for someone else's voice. The sharpest mind in the room isn't the one talking; it's the one listening so well that nothing gets missed.

Let's be honest, I bought the myth, too. For years, I mistook quick responses for wisdom. I'd plan my comeback before the question finished, thinking "leadership" meant bringing answers, not curiosity.

What I didn't see: every time I bulldozed through a conversation, hungry for my own soundbite, I missed what mattered. You end up running in circles: more talking, less trust, more "leadership energy," and way less connection.

Here's the reality check nobody likes to say out loud: The moment you stop listening, really listening, the team stops following. People don't bother speaking up if they know the conversation's just a performance. Eventually, all you hear is polite silence and checked-out minds.

You want to lead for real? Shut up and lean in. Listen so hard it costs you something. Stay open to the wild, weird, uncomfortable, even dissenting views, especially the ones that slow you down or make you question your certainty.

The bravest leaders are the ones who hand over the mic, hold the pause, and let the quietest person get to the end of their thought without stepping in.

Every time I've seen trust catch and teams start showing up for each other, it's because someone, usually the leader, finally decided to be present, not just authoritative. That's when ideas multiply. That's when people belong.

So, here's my challenge:

Stop performing "leadership listening" and start practicing presence. Don't just hear what isn't being said on the surface. Don't just lead out loud, listen out loud. Ask the question that lets someone else's story surface, then wait long enough to actually hear the answer.

If you lead with your ears, you'll be amazed at what your team builds around you. Trust follows those who truly listen.

☞ LISTENING NUGGET REFLECTION PROMPTS: LISTEN LOUDER THAN YOU LEAD

These prompts are designed to help you reflect on how you embody leadership and present yourself as a leader *before* speaking, because listening isn't what happens before you lead; it is how you lead. The more people feel heard, the more they trust your voice when it's time to use it.

Reflection Prompts

- When in conversation, am I truly present, or am I just preparing my response?

- How often do I ask deeper questions instead of giving quick answers?

- What's one moment this week where I could've listened more intentionally?

- Who in my circle may not feel heard? How can I change that?

- Do I listen to understand emotions or just collect information?

- What's one way I can slow down and truly hear someone today?

🔊 PRACTICE IT OUT LOUD: LISTEN. NOTICE. LEAD.

These are the quiet moves that make the difference. Each one helps you practice presence, build trust, and lead in ways people can feel, even before you speak.

✳ *Four-Step Guide to Practicing It Out Loud:*

1. **Check Your Default Setting**

   Before your next meeting or conversation, pause and ask: *"Am I listening to understand, or listening to reply?"* Pay attention to your body language, your pacing, and your urge to jump in.

2. **Choose One Listening Move**

   Pick one from this chapter:

   - Pause
   - Paraphrase
   - Ask an open-ended question

   Now, name the conversation where you'll try it, and notice what shifts.

3. **Invite the Unsung Voice**

   Who in your team often holds back?
   What's one way you can invite their voice today?
   Even a simple "What do you think?" Can open a door.
   Make Your Pledge

   Write out your commitment:
   "*In my next [meeting/one-on-one/call], I will_____.*"
   (Example: "In my next team huddle, I'll pause before speaking and ask, 'What's one thing we're not seeing yet?'")

✍ REFLECTION JOURNAL — BUILDING TOMORROW'S LEADERSHIP HABITS

Turn today's observations into tomorrow's leadership habits

Situation and Technique Tried	What I Noticed	What I Learned	Date

🗣 UP NEXT: EMPOWER THROUGH COMMUNICATION

You've mastered listening with intent, now it's time to speak with purpose.

In Chapter 2, you'll

- **Flip the script** from simply hearing to truly helping
- **Turn orders into ownership** with questions that spark initiative
- **Swap commands for conviction** by speaking belief into action
- **Transform everyday chats** into moments of genuine leadership

🔑 **Why it matters:** Hoarding the mic stifles potential. Real empowerment is about sharing it, and watching your team step up.

Your challenge: In your next conversation, will you wait to speak, or pass the mic?

Empowerment isn't a volume game. It's a **trust game**.

Are you ready to pass the mic? See you in Chapter 2!

EMPOWER
THROUGH
COMMUNICATION

> *"Leadership is not about being in charge. It's about taking care of those in your charge."*
>
> ~ Simon Sinek

THE LEADERSHIP MISCONCEPTION

Many leaders believe empowerment is about giving people more work, but true empowerment isn't about delegation, it's about *development*.

Empowerment is the difference between assigning a task and inspiring ownership.

When leaders use communication to elevate others, they don't just distribute responsibility; they build confidence, trust, and initiative. Empowering communication transforms passive compliance into active leadership.

WHAT IT MEANS TO EMPOWER THROUGH COMMUNICATION

Empowerment isn't about commanding; it's about inviting others to lead. It means speaking in ways that clarify expectations, encourage initiative, and build courage.

Empowering leaders use phrases like:

- *"What do you think?"*
- *"This is the vision; how can you help lead it?"*
- *"I trust your judgment; run with it."*

Empowering communication tells people:

"I see your potential, and I trust you with it."

REAL-WORLD EXAMPLE: GIVING AWAY THE MIC

When I was an Air Force leadership instructor, my role was to teach an 8-week course on every aspect of leadership, including historical, transformational, and several other concepts. What motivated me the most was teaching the young Airman who were transitioning from technical experts to Non-Commissioned-Officers who were moving to supervisory roles.

Those Airmen were brilliant and up-and-coming future leaders who often were very inquisitive. During one of our discussions, I noticed one particular Airman who was sharp and observant yet reserved. He seemed interested but rarely spoke in group discussions.

One day, I asked him directly, "Why haven't I heard from you?" His reply stuck with me, "I didn't think my opinion mattered here." His response didn't just catch me off guard; it convicted me. Not because of what he said, but because of everything I hadn't. I hadn't made space at the table or turned down my voice long enough to hear his, and in that silence, I was the one who made the room quiet.

From that point forward, I made a conscious shift. I began highlighting insights from every student, publicly affirming ideas, and inviting the quieter voices to take the lead on class discussions. By the end of the course, that same Airman was confidently leading a capstone project.

My students in that class didn't just learn leadership, they practiced it, because I stopped directing and started empowering.

📄 HISTORICAL EXAMPLE: FRANCES HESSELBEIN AND MISSION-DRIVEN EMPOWERMENT

Frances Hesselbein, former CEO of the Girl Scouts of the USA, transformed an organization known for cookies and crafts into a nationwide leadership engine for young women.

Her strategy? Empower through purpose and language.

Hesselbein did this by shifting the conversation from activity to impact. She spoke about mission, leadership, and opportunity instead of just badges and boxes. Her tone elevated the organization's self-image, and her trust in her team's potential reshaped its future.

> *"Leadership is a matter of how to be, not how to do."*
>
> ~ Frances Hesselbein

By empowering her people through vision-driven communication, she grew the organization by growing true leaders.

CONNECTION ACROSS TIME: EMPOWERING OTHERS

Looking at the two examples: the quiet Airman finding his voice, and Frances Hesselbein reshaping a century-old institution, one thing stands out. The first step for empowerment starts with words, long before it ever shows up in structure.

That Airman didn't just start speaking up; he started leading. Hesselbein created the same shift on a national scale, and her words told people they were capable, trusted, and essential. A direct result of that level of empowerment, her people led like it.

Leaders who "give away their mics" don't just change who's talking; they spark a belief in belonging. They turn spectators into stewards and silence into contribution. Powering communication sends three signals:

- **You belong.** Invitation creates safety.
- **You're needed.** Framing people in the mission or objective clearly shows why their voices matter.
- **You can lead.** Taking a moment to ask about their approach transforms them from bystanders into owners.

Language leads the culture. Slow your voice, affirm others publicly, invite quieter voices to take the lead, and you'll see the room change before the systems do.

When you tell someone, "Lead this," you're not just giving them a task. You're giving them a new story to tell about themselves; one they'll carry long after the moment ends.

🧠 CLARITY IN ACTION: ELEVATED COMMUNICATION

Want to inspire action? Speak in a way that lifts people up and unlocks their drive to lead.

Empowering communication means:

- Making your message a launchpad, not a lecture.
- Using your words to pass the mic, not hold it.
- Turning conversations into opportunities for others to shine.
- Reminding people that they don't just belong; they have roles that matter.

The most unforgettable leaders turn their words into platforms, not pedestals. You don't just lead the room, you elevate it. True empowerment is not about putting people on your shoulders.

It's about giving them roots to stand on and wings to take off, not forcing them follow your path, but allowing them to launch their own.

HOW EMPOWERING LEADERS COMMUNICATE

Leaders don't just set direction, they set tone. The words you choose can either build another leader or leave someone sitting aimlessly waiting for instructions. I've seen the difference in those critical conversations where leaders ask, "Take a swing at the plan, what would you change?" Versus others who say, "Just do it the way I showed you," which can lead to dependency. Language hands someone the keys or keeps them chained to the passenger seat. Here's how empowerment sounds, and how it doesn't.

Empowering Communication

- "What do you think?"
- "Here's the vision; how can you help lead it?"
- "I trust your judgment; run with it."
- "Let's talk about how to expand your role."

Dis-empowering Communication

- "Just do what I say."
- "That's above your pay grade."
- "I'll handle it myself."
- "Stay in your lane."

🧠 WHY PSYCHOLOGICAL SAFETY STARTS WITH SPEECH

One of the greatest predictors of team success isn't IQ or budget, it's psychological safety. People need to know they can speak up without fear of embarrassment or retribution.

Empowering communication creates that safety by:

- Encouraging questions and feedback
- Inviting dissenting opinions
- Praising in public and coaching in private
- Speaking from a place of trust, not control

⚒️ TOOLS TO EMPOWER THROUGH COMMUNICATION

- **Believe in their potential:** *"You're ready for this."*
- **Pass the mic:** Ask for their input before offering yours.
- **Frame feedback as fuel:** *"This is to build, not break."*
- **Say their name in the room:** Public recognition builds momentum.
- **Clarity = Confidence:** Be specific about roles, expectations, and goals.

🔍 CHAPTER REFLECTION: EMPOWER THROUGH COMMUNICATION

Words are weight. Every conversation is an opportunity to reinforce or diminish strength. Empowering communication means lifting others up.

Reflection Questions:

- Do people feel more confident after speaking with me?
- How often do I communicate trust, rather than just issuing instructions?
- What language habits can I change to build more leaders around me?

💡 LEADERSHIP TOOL: EMPOWERMENT CONVERSATION STARTER KIT

Use the following to launch developmental conversations and build belief.

- ☑ "What would you do in my place?"
- ☑ "What strengths do you see in yourself?"
- ☑ "Where do you want to grow and how can I help?"
- ☑ "What's something you've never been asked to lead?"
- ☑ "I see potential in you because…"

✥ CONNECTION TO THE L.E.A.D. MODEL

After listening, empowerment is the next step in the L.E.A.D. journey. It moves from understanding to uplifting. When you empower others, you multiply leadership, and that's how teams grow stronger.

Speak to develop. Communicate to empower. Lead out loud.

🎤 LEADERSHIP BONUS NUGGET #2: PASS THE MIC, NOT CONTROL

Stop performing. Start multiplying.

MYTH: The best leaders never let go of the microphone. They need to be the voice, the authority, the one everyone watches, the star of the show.

TRUTH: You want the truth? The tighter you grip the mic, the quieter your team gets. I learned that the hard way. Every time I dominated the conversation, there was this slow silence that crept across the table. It wasn't respect, it was resignation. Turns out, when you're always the loudest, the only thing you amplify is your own fear: the fear that if you don't fill the air, nobody else will.

Here is something you don't hear until you go to strategic-level leadership school: Power isn't hoarded, it's handed off. When you pass the mic and mean it, something wild happens; people step up. They don't just echo, they create. You go from conducting solos to building a symphony. The team stops waiting for your verdict and starts inventing music you'd never have dreamed up alone.

Real empowerment isn't just about tossing tasks at people; it's about inviting their ideas and hearing their voice, even when it wobbles. It's trusting that if you step back a little, the song gets bigger, bolder, a little more alive.

I'll never forget the first time I let someone else give direction while I sat in the back row, sweating more than any speech I've ever given, but when their voice rang out, the room leaned in. I realized what actual leadership felt like, not performing, but distributing, multiplying what matters.

If you want a team that moves mountains, stop being the boulder at the top. Let others reach the summit. When you share the mic, you start a movement, not a monologue.

So, pass the mic. Build a symphony, not a solo. Let them lead the song you started, and watch how the music keeps going, even after you put your mic down.

⌐⊙ LEADERSHIP NUGGET REFLECTION PROMPTS: PASS THE MIC, NOT CONTROL

These prompts are designed to help you reflect on how you use communication to build others up, not just to inform, but to empower. Real leadership doesn't just speak; it *creates space for others to lead too.*

Reflection Prompts

1. When I communicate, do I invite others to lead, or do I just ask them to listen?

2. What's one conversation where I passed the mic, and what happened because of it?

3. Do people feel trusted after talking with me, or just tasked?

4. How often do I speak belief into someone's potential before they see it themselves?

5. Where might I still be holding on to control out of fear, not wisdom?

6. What's one way I gave someone ownership and the voice to go with it, this week?

✏ PRACTICE IT OUT LOUD: PASS THE MIC, NOT THE CONTROL

These are the intentional leadership moves that multiply trust. Each one helps you shift from speaking to developing, from leading alone to building leaders around you.

✳ *Four-Step Guide to Practicing It Out Loud*

1. **Watch Your Words**

   Take note of a recent phrase you used. Was it controlling ("I'll handle it"), or empowering ("I trust your judgment")?

2. **Ask Before You Answer**

   The next time someone brings you a question, pause. Ask:
   "What do you think?"
   You'll often find they already have the answer and just need the courage to own it.

3. **Expand the Circle**

   Who haven't you given leadership space to yet? What's one way you can invite them into a role, a decision, or a conversation this week?

4. **Speak the Trust Out Loud**

Write your commitment:
"In my next [meeting/1-on-1/project], I will empower by saying_____."
(Example: "I trust your instincts, run with it, and I'll support you along the way.")

📔 REFLECTION JOURNAL — BUILD TOMORROW'S LEADERSHIP HABITS

Turn today's empowerment into tomorrow's leadership opportunities

Use this space to capture moments where you communicated in ways that empowered others, where you made space instead of taking control.

What shifted? How did people respond? What did you learn about your leadership voice?

Date	Situation + Phrase Used	What You Learned or Noticed

UP NEXT: ADAPT AND OVERCOME

You've passed the mic; now you need to adjust the sails.

In Chapter 3, we'll

- **Step into the storm**, trading comfort for courage and rigid plans for resilient pivots
- **Steer your team through chaos** with honest, bite-sized updates that cut through confusion.
- **Anchor your presence,** so calm confidence replaces panic and uncertainty

Pause now, and your momentum stalls.

Lean in, and your team finds its compass.

Your challenge: When the winds shift, will you cling to the blueprint or master your pivot?

Leadership isn't about flawless plans; it's about **carrying strength through the storm**.

Are you ready to adjust your sails? See you in Chapter 3!

ADAPT AND OVERCOME

> *"In preparing for battle, I have always found that plans are useless, but planning is indispensable."*
>
> ~ Dwight D. Eisenhower

THE LEADERSHIP MISCONCEPTION

There's a saying I grew up hearing: *"A good captain goes down with the ship, but a great captain sees danger and adjusts his sails."*

Too often, people believe leadership is about creating a perfect plan and sticking to it, no matter what. However, that's not leadership, that's stubbornness disguised as strategy.

Real leadership is rooted in the mission but flexible in the method. It's not about change for the sake of change. It's about staying present, reading the environment, and being ready to pivot with clarity and courage.

Adaptability is seeing the problem and adjusting the sails so your crew can avoid or minimize any danger. It's anticipating the impact and communicating the shift, keeping the ship afloat and your people confident in the journey ahead.

ADAPTABILITY IS A COMMUNICATION SKILL

If leadership is about adjusting your sails, communication is about how you steer. Your ability to adapt starts with how you guide others, how you speak when plans shift, how you lead when conditions change, and how you keep your people informed in real time.

Adaptability resides in your voice long before it manifests in your actions. When the unexpected hits, your team needs steady, honest communication that helps them stay oriented and confident.

Inflexible Leadership

- The Flag Planter Leader: "Stick to the plan, no changes."
- The Fire and Forget Leader: Communicates once, then disappears
- The One-Size-Fits-All Leader: Same message for everyone
- The Panicker: Reacts emotionally in times of uncertainty

Adaptive Leadership

- "Here's the mission and here's how we'll adjust if needed."
- Shares consistent updates with context
- Tailor's delivery based on the situation and the audience
- Responds with focus, calm, and clarity

☑ REAL-WORLD EXAMPLE: LEADING AFTER THE STORM

Years ago, in the southern U.S., a category-five hurricane struck, and one particular Air Force base was hit hard. I volunteered alongside a small team to help stabilize the area. We arrived to find systems down, buildings damaged, and people emotionally drained.

There was no playbook, just people looking for guidance. So, we committed to communicating *constantly*.

We gathered for daily huddles, shifted plans by the hour, and made space for every voice. We didn't pretend to have all the answers, but we made sure no one felt left in the dark.

Every update was a stabilizer. Every honest answer built trust. Slowly, systems came online, morale lifted, and what started as survival turned into momentum. Adaptability, paired with communication, became our anchor.

📄 HISTORICAL EXAMPLE: WINSTON CHURCHILL LEADING THROUGH THE STORM

In 1940, as Nazi Germany expanded across Europe, many British citizens braced for what felt like inevitable defeat, but Prime Minister Winston Churchill refused to give up.

Churchill carefully adjusted how he spoke to the nation. Through clear and confident broadcasts, Churchill provided the public with structure, hope, and purpose. His voice, steady, bold, and unyielding, became the message: "We shall fight on the beaches… we shall never surrender."

He gave his people stability and presence. That made all the difference.

CONNECTION ACROSS TIME: CONTROL YOUR SIGNAL

Churchill's wartime resolve and our hurricane recovery shared one thing: clarity in chaos.

When you can't control the storm, you can still control what you say, how you say it, and how effectively you lead.

CLARITY THROUGH CHAOS:

During disruption, your team doesn't expect or need perfection; they need presence.

Communicate the following three things clearly:

1. What we know

2. What we're doing

3. What comes next

This structure calms anxiety and replaces confusion with direction.

TOOLS TO COMMUNICATE WHILE ADAPTING

These tools will help you adapt and communicate through any situation.

- **Command the message:** Stick to 2–3 key points and repeat them often.

- **Stay visible:** Leadership isn't just decisions, it's presence.

- **Mix delivery channels:** Use in-person, email, visual, and voice.

- **Ask for feedback:** Asking "What's unclear right now?" Opens the door for feedback.

- **Signal confidence, not perfection:** "Here's what we know, and we can adjust as needed."

🔍 CHAPTER REFLECTION: ADAPT AND OVERCOME

Adaptability is often viewed as a reaction, but it is also a relational tool. It shows up in the unknown, through presence, voice, and clarity.

Reflection Questions:

1. How do I show up when plans fall apart?

2. Do I lead with clarity, or contribute to confusion?

3. How can I prepare my team for disruption before it happens?

💬 Lead through the storm. Speak stability. Adapt out loud.

☁ BONUS LEADERSHIP NUGGET #3: BE THE "STORM-BEARER" NOT THE "STORM-BRINGER"

Turn Storms to Strength

MYTH: When the heat is on, real leaders crank up the volume, push harder, get louder, take control, and show everyone who's boss.

TRUTH: The strongest leader in the storm isn't the one shouting orders; it's the one who walks in steady, keeps their heartbeat slow, and refuses to throw more lightning into an already wild sky. You want to help your team? Carry the storm, don't add to it.

I'll level with you: In my first few rounds with crisis, I thought "leadership" meant bringing thunder. I scheduled emergency meetings, raised my voice, powered through stress by dialing up the intensity, thinking that if I just fought harder, I could force things back into place, but chaos doesn't bow to aggression; it feeds off it. Most of the time, all I did was turn a storm into a hurricane. My team didn't need a bigger weather system; they needed a lighthouse.

Here's the leadership lesson, nobody taught me: When you show up with storm energy, you multiply the mess. If you're the loudest voice in the room, you're not calming them; you're just raising their blood pressure. Your people don't need someone to out-yell the problem; they need someone who makes the room feel safer the second you walk in.

Being a "storm-bearer" isn't about pretending the storm isn't real. It means you absorb some of that chaos and let your steady presence anchor the panic. You become the eye of the hurricane, the calm, the perspective, the "we got this even if it hurts," not another set of hands throwing more debris into the air.

Real strength isn't measured by how much pressure you apply in a crunch; it's measured by how much pressure you can absorb without transmitting it to everyone around you. The leaders who earn trust are the ones who can take a hit and still help others dance in the rain.

When the next crisis hits and your instinct is to take the room by force, do something different. Step slower. Drop your voice. Ground yourself. Ask: "How can I be the anchor right now?"

Don't hide in your office, show up in the mess, but show up steady, not spiked.

When everything shakes, be the thing that stands. That's how storms turn into strength, and that's the kind of leader people gladly follow through the thunder.

☁ Leadership Nugget Reflection Prompts: Be the Storm-Bearer

These prompts are designed to help you reflect on how you present yourself when everything around you is in flux. Being adaptable isn't about bracing for chaos; it's about *carrying calm through it.* Your voice can be the anchor, even when your surroundings are uncertain, because when storms come, leaders don't shrink back; they show up stronger.

Reflection Prompts

1. When pressure hits, do I respond with presence or react from panic?

2. How do I ground myself when everything around me is shifting?

3. What's the one storm I've weathered, and what strength did it reveal in me?

4. How do I help others find clarity when the path isn't clear?

5. Where might I be holding too tightly to control instead of leading with calmness?

6. What would it look like to carry strength instead of stress this week?

☁ Practice It Out Loud: Be the Storm-Bearer

These are the steady moves that help you lead through disruption. Each one helps you reset your posture, quiet the panic, and lead with clarity under pressure.

✳ *Four-Step Guide to Practicing It Out Loud*

1. **Scan for Storm Signals**

   Think of a time this week when you felt tension rising, on your team, in a conversation, or inside yourself. How did you respond? What message did your tone and posture send?

2. **Anchor with Your Words**

   Choose one phrase to keep ready in high-stakes moments.
   (Examples: "Here's what we know." / "Let's take one step at a time." / "I've got you.")
   Use it when emotions rise and notice how others respond.

3. **Model the Reset**

   When you feel your own anxiety spike, pause. Take 10 seconds. Reframe the moment. Say out loud, "Let's take a pause. Now, let's solve this puzzle one piece at a time." Show your team that resets are a strength, not a weakness.

4. **Commit to Calm Leadership**

   Write your pledge:
   "In my next [briefing/team meeting/tough moment], I will show up with_____."
   (Example: "In my next team meeting, I will speak slowly, offer three clear next steps, and hold space for questions.")

📖 REFLECTION JOURNAL – BUILD TOMORROW'S LEADERSHIP HABITS

Turn pressure into presence by practicing grounded leadership

Use this space to capture moments where your adaptability shaped the tone of the room and gave your team direction during the storm.

Date	Disruption/ Shift	What I Modeled	What You Noticed/ Learned

UP NEXT: DECIDE AND DELIVER

You've weathered the storm; now it's time to turn the wheel.

In Chapter 4, we're leaving the comfort zone behind. It's time to move from reacting to leading, from uncertainty to action.

You'll learn how to:

- **Decide with clarity,** cut through the noise and lead forward
- **Turn hesitation into momentum,** move when others freeze
- **Anchor your team** with bold choices not perfect plans

Here's the cost of waiting: opportunities vanish, momentum dies, and teams lose faith when leaders freeze.

Here's your challenge: When the moment calls, will you freeze, or step up and lead with guts and grit?

True leadership isn't about waiting for perfection. It's about showing up bold, moving when it matters, and letting your actions do the talking.

The helm is yours; are you ready to move?

Meet me in Chapter 4.

DECIDE AND DELIVER

> *"In any moment of decision, the best thing you can do is the right thing, the next best thing is the wrong thing, and the worst thing is nothing."*
>
> ~ Theodore Roosevelt

🔍 THE LEADERSHIP MISCONCEPTION

Too many leaders believe that leadership is about waiting for perfect data, total agreement, or complete certainty. However, leadership isn't defined by perfection; it's defined by movement.

Indecision creates confusion. Action creates clarity.

You can't lead without making decisions, and even more importantly, you must deliver these decisions with strength, speed, and purpose.

✺ THE FOUR STAGES OF EVERY DECISION

1. Gather input, weigh the risks, and consider potential outcomes
2. Make the decision
3. Deliver it with purpose
4. Explain the decision with clarity, context, and conviction

Even the best decision will fall flat if the delivery is:

- Confusing — people won't know what to do
- Tentative — people won't believe you're sure

- Poorly timed — people won't act fast enough

Great leaders don't just decide. They own the decision and deliver it with presence.

☑ REAL-WORLD EXAMPLE: LEADING WITH SPEED AND CLARITY

During one of my most complex assignments as an Air Force Non-Commissioned Officer, my department was hit with a sudden budget cut. Two major programs, both critical to our mission, were suddenly at risk. The team needed direction, and there was no time for drawn-out analysis.

So, I called a rapid huddle, laid out the facts, clearly presented the options, and then made the call.

Next, I did what mattered most: I delivered the "why."

I explained the impact, the rationale, and the steps ahead. I didn't sugarcoat the trade-offs, but I did lead with confidence and transparency.

That one decision turned what could have been frustration into focus. The team rallied, trust surged, and execution followed.

It wasn't the perfect decision, but it was a clear one.

When the stakes are high, making a decision can tip the scales from failure to success.

📄 HISTORICAL EXAMPLE: JOHN F. KENNEDY (JFK) AND THE CUBAN MISSILE CRISIS

In October 1962, President John F. Kennedy faced a crisis that could have triggered global catastrophe: Soviet nuclear missiles, newly discovered on the island of Cuba.

Military, political, and public voices demanded speedy action, often war, but Kennedy refused to be rushed or carried away by panic, or by pride.

Instead, he created space for honest debate. He asked hard questions. He pressed his advisers for alternatives, and when the moment came, he made the call, not for war, but for a naval blockade, delivering an ultimatum, and opening a path out of the deadlock.

Kennedy didn't hide from the nation. He explained his decision, its risks, and his reasoning, so clearly that the entire world could hear. Privately, he prepared to carry the blame, should it all go wrong.

> *"Whether you get good advice or bad advice, the decision is yours alone," JFK reflected afterward.*

Most of us will never face such epic stakes. But we will all have moments when the world feels on the brink, and all eyes are on us to decide and deliver.

The lesson? Don't wait for perfect safety. Own your responsibility. Ask the right questions. And have the courage not just to decide, but to deliver your reasoning openly, even when the heat is on.

CONNECTION ACROSS TIME

Not every decision will make history or have worldwide implications, as displayed in JFK's decision during the Cuban Missile Crisis, where the world waited for his call. Yet, every great leader knows what those high-stakes feelings are like, when all eyes are looking to you for leadership and guidance. There are no magical timeouts or pause buttons, and waiting isn't an option.

Though most of us won't face that magnitude of risk, you must remember the stakes are always real to the people in the room with us. When a budget cut hit my team, there was no time to wait for perfect answers, but there's always room for honest ones. I called a rapid huddle to pull my team in close, laid out the facts, made the hard call, and, most importantly, explained the "why." That decision will not be written in world history books or global magazines, but it settled nerves, sparked trust, and got us moving.

Whether it's a global standoff or a team caught between panic and decision, leadership is demanded in those delicate moments between panic and action. People don't crave perfection; they need presence and clarity to get them through.

CLARITY IN ACTION: LEADING THROUGH UNCERTAINTY

Clarity is what makes change manageable.

When things shift, don't go silent.

Instead, say:

- "Here's what's changing, and why."
- "Here's how we're responding."
- "Here's what you can do next."

When leaders communicate with presence and purpose; uncertainty becomes a path instead of a barrier.

THE 4 C'S OF DECISION DELIVERY

Principle	What It Sounds Like
Clarity	"This is the decision. Here's what it means."
Context	"Here's why we're doing this."
Confidence	"I stand by this, and here's what's next.
Consistency	"You'll hear from me again on [date/time]."

When these four are present, even tough decisions gain traction and trust.

TOOLS TO DECIDE AND DELIVER

Delivering tough decisions comes with many challenges, please use these tools to help in that process.

- **Commander's or Leader's intent** – Define what success looks like, not just the task.

- **Explain the why** – Tie it to mission, values, and impact.

- **Own the outcome** – Take responsibility, whether it succeeds or not.

- **Open feedback channels** – Allow space for input after the decision.

- **Set the next checkpoint** – Let people know when they'll hear from you again.

🔍 CHAPTER REFLECTION: DECIDE AND DELIVER

Leadership gets loud in moments of decision. This is when people look to you. This is when trust is either earned or lost.

Reflection Questions:

- When was the last time I hesitated to make a decision? What did it cost?

- Do I clearly explain my "why" when communicating decisions?

- How can I make my next big decision with more clarity and conviction?

⚡ LEADERSHIP TOOL: DECISION CLARITY CHECKLIST

- ☑ Did I gather enough input from key stakeholders?
- ☑ Is the decision aligned with mission and values?
- ☑ Do I understand short- and long-term consequences?
- ☑ Am I ready to communicate the "why"?
- ☑ Have I picked the right time and method to deliver it?
- ☑ Do people know the next step and who is responsible for it?

📊 RAPID DECISION MATRIX

Use this matrix when under pressure:

High Impact - Irreversible	Low Impact - Reversible
Pause briefly, Gather Input, Then Act	Delegate & Decide
Decide & Communicate the "Why"	Gather Buy-In, Then Decide
Decide & Be Present	Decide & Correct as Needed

💡 Tip: Most decisions are reversible. Don't let fear of imperfection block momentum.

🧩 CONNECTION TO THE L.E.A.D. MODEL

"Decide and Deliver" is where everything comes together. After you've listened, empowered, and adapted, this is the moment your leadership voice becomes real.

A strong, clearly-delivered decision anchors your credibility.

Decide boldly. Deliver clearly. Lead forward.

⚙️ BONUS LEADERSHIP NUGGET #4: BE THE VOICE BEFORE THE VOID

Make the Call, Before the Silence Does.

MYTH: Great leaders stay silent until everything's certain. If you don't have the answers, it's better to keep quiet and look wise.

TRUTH: I've learned the hard way: silence in a crisis isn't tactical, it's abandonment. When you don't speak, the room fills up with worry, gossip, and guesses. Chaos loves a vacuum, and your silence gives it power.

Let's be real, I've frozen before. I thought waiting meant I was protecting my people from bad news, or maybe just buying time. Truth is, every minute I held back made things heavier for everyone. People don't sit calmly in silence. They fill the gap with their fears, and usually, the worst-case scenario wins.

You might think you're being careful, but really, you're just letting anxiety do all the talking. I've watched trust fray, momentum stall, and teams drift apart, all because a leader (usually me) got too quiet, too careful, too obsessed with certainty that never came.

It doesn't take perfect answers; it takes presence. Sometimes what your team needs is someone willing to say, "I don't have it all yet, but here's what we do know, and here's where we'll move next." That, messy as it sounds, is often the anchor people need when things get foggy.

Your voice, even unsteady, is still a signal in the storm. Every call you make when it's hard is a brick in the wall of trust. Delay too long, and every silent minute chips away at what you've built.

So, when the air's thick and you can almost hear the temperature rising, don't sit at your desk waiting for perfect. Go first. Open your mouth. Let your team see you, not just your memo.

Make the call before silence does. Step in before the void gets louder than you.

Be the voice before the void. Trust isn't built in the moments you've got all the answers; it's forged when you speak up anyway, even if your voice shakes. That's what true leadership sounds like.

📣 Leadership Nugget Reflection Prompts: Be the Voice Before the Void

These prompts are designed to help you reflect on how you show up when decisions need to be made, not just with information, but with intention, because in moments of silence, leaders speak.

Reflection Prompts

1. What decisions have I been avoiding, and what's it costing me or my team?

2. Do I over-process in search of certainty, or trust myself to lead through clarity?

3. When was the last time I made a hard call and stood by it, what did I learn?

4. How do I explain the *why* behind my decisions?

5. What impact does my indecision have on those who look to me for direction?

6. Where can I give my team more confidence through clear, timely action this week?

Practice It Out Loud: Decide. Deliver. Anchor.

These moments of clarity aren't just about making decisions; they're about moving with purpose. Use this guide to activate bold, aligned action.

✳ *Four-Step Guide to Practicing It Out Loud:*

1. **Notice the Stall Point**

    What decision are you delaying out of fear of not having the whole picture?
    Pinpoint the moment where progress paused.

2. **Check for Alignment**

    What's the mission, and what matters most?
    Align your decision to the greater why, then simplify the message.

3. **Choose Your Delivery Method**

    How will you deliver it, via a team meeting, one-on-one, email, or call?
    Pick the method that brings the most clarity and connection.

4. **Make the Call, Then Stay Present**

    Don't just drop the message and go. Be visible. Stay engaged.
    "In my next [brief/team talk/email], I will clearly state the decision and the reason behind it."

📖 REFLECTION JOURNAL — BUILDING TOMORROW'S LEADERSHIP HABITS

Turn today's clarity into tomorrow's consistency

Use this space to capture the moments where you didn't just wait, you led. What decision did you make that moved things forward? How did you bring others with you through your communication? What was the shift, internal or external, that signaled it was time to act?

Leadership doesn't wait for the perfect moment. It creates it. Let this page remind you that momentum often begins with a single, clear choice.

Date	Disruption/ Activity	What I Communicated	What You Noticed/ Learned

🗣 UP NEXT: THE VOICE OF INFLUENCE

You've made the call, now you must champion its impact.

In Chapter 5, you will

- **Anchor your decisions** in clarity so every directive resonates
- **Speak with presence** that can turn any announcements into action
- **Command attention** from the quietest huddle to the largest boardroom
- **Tie choices to conviction** so your voice outlives the echo

🔑 **Your challenge:** After your next decision, will you let it drift, or will you carry that conviction into every conversation?

Influence is not earned by volume; it's forged in **purposeful presence**.

Let's carry that conviction into Chapter 5!

THE VOICE OF INFLUENCE

> *"The art of communication is the language of leadership."*
>
> ~ James Humes

🔍 THE LEADERSHIP MISCONCEPTION

There is a common misconception that all leaders speak with big, loud, commanding voices. You know, the kind of voices that fill a room, so big that when they speak, everyone listens. **This is simply a myth, born of historical leadership dogma.**

Your voice is your leadership signature. Whether you're leading a meeting, giving a briefing, or mentoring a teammate, how you speak influences how others respond, immediately and over time. You don't need to be loud or flashy to be powerful. You just need to be intentional.

👤 What Makes a Voice Influential?

Have you ever wondered what makes a voice impactful or influential? If so, these are some core principles that can help.

- **Clarity** – Clear words, focused message, logical flow
- **Confidence** – A steady tone that reflects self-belief and command
- **Connection** – Eye contact, natural gestures, presence
- **Conviction** – Passion moves people from hearing to acting

These qualities aren't reserved for keynote speakers. They're daily tools for effective leadership.

THE SCIENCE BEHIND VOCAL INFLUENCE

Studies suggest that tone, pace, and delivery can dramatically impact how your message is received, sometimes even more than the words themselves.

Research by Dr. Albert Mehrabian found that when conveying feelings or attitudes:

- 7% of meaning comes from words
- 38% from tone of voice
- 55% from body language

While these figures don't apply to all communication, they highlight a crucial truth: how you deliver your message matters deeply, especially in emotionally charged or high-stakes moments.

When you own your voice, you increase engagement, reduce miscommunication, and elevate team performance. Your voice is strategy.

REAL-WORLD EXAMPLE: COMMANDING THE ROOM WITH CLARITY

As an Air Force Senior Non-Commissioned Officer and team leader, I was once asked to present at a multinational briefing attended by numerous diplomats and senior military officials. The financial update we were asked to present was complex, the meeting was high-stakes, and the notice was short. A trifecta of adversity.

Instead of rushing and giving in to the urge to hide behind technical jargon, we met the adversity with calm. As we presented, we slowed our pace, used deliberate pauses, and delivered each point with clarity and presence. Clean visuals supported our words, but the real power came from how we spoke.

Partway through the presentation, we watched as confusion gave way to nods and doubt gave way to trust. What started as just another financial report turned into a leadership moment. We were invited to return for future briefings because we successfully delivered clarity and confidence.

Your voice can unlock doors, no matter the topic or audience.

📄 HISTORICAL EXAMPLE: MARTIN LUTHER KING JR. AND THE POWER OF DELIVERY

Dr. Martin Luther King Jr.'s "I Have a Dream" speech stands as a masterclass in influential communication, often remembered not just for its words, but for the way those words were brought to life. Dr. King wielded his voice like an instrument, rising and falling with conviction and compassion, each pause amplifying the weight of his message.

Through deliberate cadence, repetition, "I have a dream," and raw emotion, he forged a rhythm that unified a nation's hopes and ignited the hearts of millions. He didn't merely recite lines; he embodied vision, turning personal conviction into collective momentum.

What set Dr. King apart wasn't just his authority; it was the authenticity burning through every word. His passion and presence turned a speech into a rallying cry and a moment into a movement. Dr. King reminds us: real leadership doesn't just speak to minds, it moves hearts, sparks action, and echoes through generations

CONNECTION ACROSS TIME

What Dr. King did with a microphone, we all have the power to do in our daily leadership roles. You don't need a stage. Your team, your client, your community, they are all your audience.

How you deliver your message will decide whether it lands or gets lost.

When you speak with presence, clarity, and conviction, your influence expands far beyond the words themselves.

CLARITY IN ACTION: SPEAK LIKE YOU LEAD

Before your next meeting, plan your points and plan your presence.

Ask:

- What emotions do I want to evoke?
- Where will I pause for impact?
- What sentence will I deliver with conviction?

Next, rehearse out loud, because your voice carries leadership.

🛠 TOOLS TO STRENGTHEN YOUR VOICE OF INFLUENCE

- **Vocal warm-ups** – Try humming, breathing deeply, or tongue twisters before speaking.
- **Power poses** – Use open, grounded posture to boost confidence before high-stakes conversations.
- **Pace & pause** – Avoid speaking too fast. Use silence for emphasis.
- **Tone variation** – Shift your pitch and volume to maintain engagement.
- **Eye contact** – Speak to individuals in the room, not just the group.
- **Storytelling** – Anchor key points to relatable, emotional stories.

🔍 CHAPTER REFLECTION: THE VOICE OF INFLUENCE

Your voice is a reflection of your intention. What you emphasize, how you pause, and the passion in your tone, all communicate your mindset before your message.

Reflection Questions:

- Does my voice reflect the leader I want to be?
- Do I speak with clarity or clutter?
- What habits can I adopt to improve my vocal presence this week?
- How do my tone and body language shape trust?

💡 LEADERSHIP TOOL: DAILY VOCAL PREP CHECKLIST

- ☑ 1-minute grounding breath
- ☑ 30 seconds of vocal warm-up (tongue twisters, lip rolls)
- ☑ Confident posture or power stance
- ☑ Choose one phrase you'll deliver with impact today
- ☑ Use 15 seconds of silence before a key interaction to reset your presence

✿ CONNECTION TO THE L.E.A.D. MODEL.

Your voice carries every piece of your leadership:

- It listens before it speaks.
- It empowers through clarity.
- It adapts based on the moment.
- It delivers with presence.

To lead out loud is to speak with purpose. Your voice conveys information *and* inspiration.

🔭 BONUS LEADERSHIP NUGGET #5: LIGHT THE VISION, DON'T JUST CAST IT

Don't Just Say the Words, Let People Feel the Spark

MYTH: Vision comes from the stage, a big announcement, some grand mission statement, a few spotlight moments with the boss at the mic. Shout it loud enough and watch people fall in line.

TRUTH: If your people can only find the vision on a PowerPoint, you're already behind. Real vision doesn't echo from the top; it burns at the center. If your team can't see themselves in what you're building, it doesn't matter how many all-hands you call or how polished your speech is. Empty words never started a movement.

I'll be honest: I've stood at the front of the room, voice hoarse from rallying the troops. I thought if the words were strong, I'd see eyes light up, but most folks were waiting for the meeting to end.

What I missed, and what most leaders miss, is that vision only works if people stop feeling like passengers and start acting like architects. If you want buy-in, you must give them blueprints and let them put their fingerprints on the plan.

Ever notice how the best teams never quote the poster on the wall, but can all tell you what they're building and why it keeps them up at night? The missing piece isn't volume, it's conviction. It's the difference between noise and a bonfire.

If your team doesn't believe in the "why," you're just casting fog; they'll drift, wait for cues, and play it safe, but when folks feel like their name is somewhere on the cornerstone, everything shifts. They sweat, stretch, and scrap for what matters. They stop asking "Is this my job?" And start moving as if it's their mission.

Here's the challenge that I now constantly give myself: Before I finish any vision talk, I ask, "If I said nothing tomorrow, would they build anyway?" If the answer's no, I know I need to hand over the torch, not just talk about where it's going.

Don't waste vision on scripts and slides. Make it real enough to raise goosebumps, urgent enough that nobody can sit still. Get so clear you make the future feel possible, and so contagious you don't need to push, because your people are already pulling you.

Vision isn't wallpaper. It's wildfire, one spark, passed hand to hand. Stop casting wallpaper. Light it. Then get out of the way and watch them turn it into something you never could have built alone.

Don't just cast vision, light it. Burn it in, pass it on, and watch what happens when your team stops waiting for permission and starts building what matters. That's how you start a movement.

◻️ Leadership Nugget Reflection Prompts: LIGHT THE VISION, DON'T JUST CAST IT

These prompts are designed to help you reflect on how you communicate vision, not as a directive, but as an invitation. The goal isn't just to be believed, but to be followed with purpose.

Reflection Prompts

1. Do the people I lead feel like they're part of the mission, or just following orders?

2. When was the last time I made our vision personal, not just professional?

3. What's one way I've lived the vision this week through action, not just explanation?

4. How often do I connect today's task to tomorrow's impact?

5. What language do I use when casting vision? Does it ignite belief or just deliver facts?

6. Who needs to hear the "why" behind what we're doing today?

⊛ Practice It Out Loud: Ignite. Align. Embody.

Vision isn't just something you say, it's something you model. The best leaders validate their belief in that vision every day by the way they act, speak, and follow through. However, with ineffective leaders, you won't have to ask if they believe in their vision, as it's usually clear that their vision is just words on paper. There's no follow-through, conviction, or belief in any of their actions.

It must be something that burns so brightly in you that everyone around you can feel the warmth of that future state.

Please use this guide to activate alignment, belief, and energy in real time.

✳ *Four-Step Guide to Practicing It Out Loud:*

1. **Define the "Why Behind the Work"**

   Pick one goal, challenge, or initiative you're leading. Why does it matter, beyond the metrics?

2. **Find the Story Behind the Strategy**

   What story can you tell that emotionally connects people to the vision? It could be your own, a teammate's, or a client's experience.

3. **Make It Personal and Visible**

   How are you modeling belief in the vision?
   Is your tone, effort, and presence matching the future you're calling others to?

4. **Light One Spark**

   Choose one person to have a vision-centered conversation with this week.
   "In my next [huddle, one-on-one, team call], I'll connect what we're doing to why it matters, and who it's for."

📓 REFLECTION JOURNAL – BUILDING TOMORROW'S LEADERSHIP HABITS

Turn today's sparks into lasting vision habits

Use this space to document how you've brought the vision to life, not just in what you said, but how you showed up. What moment lit the spark? Who responded? What did it teach you about belief and alignment?

Date	Vision Shared	How It Was Received	What Shifted or Sparked

🗣 UP NEXT: MASTERING CONNECTION THROUGH STORYTELLING

You've sharpened your voice, now you get to spark belief.

In Chapter 6, you'll

- **Pick the right character** so people see themselves in your story
- **Frame real conflict** that raises the stakes and stirs emotion
- **Highlight the turning point** that shifts mindsets and fuels action
- **Close with purpose** so your audience knows exactly what to do next

🔑 *Pause here, and you risk becoming just another data dump.*

Lean into the story, and you ignite trust and momentum.

Your challenge: In your very next communication, lead with a story, not a stat.

Ready to be the story they can't forget?

Let's carry that conviction into Chapter 6!

MASTERING CONNECTION THROUGH STORYTELLING

> *"Stories constitute the single most powerful weapon in a leader's arsenal."*
>
> ~ Howard Gardner

THE LEADERSHIP MISCONCEPTION

Many people assume that storytelling is just for professional stages or bedtime routines. Long before presentations and PowerPoint, storytelling was a matter of life and death. Dating back over 30,000 years, early humans used stories to share life-saving knowledge such as how to spot danger, when to move, what to avoid, and how to thrive together. These were tales, but also important tools.

Today, storytelling still serves that purpose. For leaders, the goal is to convey the message clearly enough for action. Clarity is the modern survival skill. It's what turns information into alignment and direction into momentum.

The best leaders don't just speak, they simplify. They translate strategy into action with clarity at the core.

When information is delivered as a story, we lean in. We remember. We act. In leadership, clear message design is one of the most practical communication tools you can utilize.

You can have the right strategy, the best data, and the most motivated team, but if your message is confusing, it won't move anyone. Action always has clarity at the core.

📖 WHY STORIES MATTER

Stories give your leadership voice depth and dimension.

They:

- Connect people to purpose
- Humanize your message
- Inspire action through emotion

As a leader, your job is not to just tell people what to do. Your job is to tell them *why it matters*. Stories accomplish this better than any slide, stat, or slogan ever could.

🗝️ ELEMENTS OF A POWERFUL LEADERSHIP STORY

We throw around the word masterclass like it's a badge you can buy, but absolute mastery in leadership storytelling isn't about a fancy label.

It's about earning the right to be remembered.

If you want your stories to stick, really stick, you've got to build them with the elements that pull people in and make it almost impossible to leave without knowing how it ends. Have you ever been watching a very interesting feed and it refreshes before you reach the end? The rest of the day or night, you stuck wondering.

A masterclass story is just that. A great story makes people think, feel, and move. So, what's the secret?

It's not more drama, it's more design.

Here's how to build it:

- ☑ **Relatable character** – People want to see themselves in the story
- ☑ **Clear conflict** – What was at stake? What needed to be overcome?
- ☑ **Turning point** – What changed? What decision shifted the course?
- ☑ **Resolution** – What was the outcome or lesson learned?
- ☑ **Call to action** – What do you want the audience to do or believe as a result of this message?

☑ REAL-WORLD EXAMPLE: TURNING ADVERSITY INTO IDENTITY

During a leadership seminar a few years ago, I was about to address a room filled with Airmen. I had planned to start my talk with some statistics and data from the field, but as I glanced into the audience, I realized that I wanted to start the day stronger.

I wanted to humanize my connection to the Airmen in the audience. So, I started with a story.

I shared my story of a time when I was leading a team that was in charge of recovery efforts after a devastating event. Instead of dwelling on the destruction, I framed it as a defining moment that we "got to" overcome.

I described the exhaustion and determination on my team's faces, the long nights filled with uncertainty, and the small victories that sustained us.

I demonstrated how a handful of Airmen, through unity, grit, and relentless commitment, transformed their squadron into the top-rated Comptroller Squadron in the Air Force that year.

You could feel the positive energy in the room. People didn't just hear my story, they felt it, and then something remarkable happened: they started sharing their own stories of hardship. Stories of resilience. Stories of leadership forged in fire.

Stories aren't fluff. They're fuel.

📄 HISTORICAL EXAMPLE: NELSON MANDELA AND THE STORY OF UNITY

When Nelson Mandela became President of South Africa after decades of apartheid and imprisonment, the nation was bitterly divided, racially, politically, and emotionally.

Instead of retaliating or issuing grand decrees, Mandela used stories to connect.

He often shared personal accounts of fellow prisoners, compassionate guards, and communities that chose forgiveness over vengeance.

One of his most powerful leadership moments came during the 1995 Rugby World Cup. Mandela rallied a divided country by telling a story of national unity and wearing the jersey of the Springboks, a historically white team.

This was a symbolic and significant gesture that told millions of people "We are one nation. We rise together."

Rather than avoiding pain, Mandela acknowledged it, re-framing the pain as a story that pointed toward hope and healing.

Nelson Mandela's leadership reminds us that while a powerful story doesn't erase the past, it can redefine the future.

🔗 CONNECTION ACROSS TIME: STORYTELLING CONNECTS GENERATIONS

When Nelson Mandela used a story to unify a divided South Africa, he proved that a strong narrative could do what mandates cannot: build trust, foster identity, and move people forward together.

You can also use storytelling to unite a team.

In every organization, there are moments of disconnection, fatigue, or friction. And in those moments, while facts alone won't move people, stories will.

A well-told story of a challenge overcome, a mission lived out, or a value embodied can realign teams and rekindle belief.

Storytelling connects emotion to action, past to future, and people to purpose.

You don't need a podium, a global spotlight, or a million viewers watching your social media live-stream. All you need to use are the stories you already have that demonstrate growth, adversity, and triumph.

One of the first stories ever told was how we used to live, chickens being thrown over our heads to treat chicken pox as kids. These simple stories serve as connectors and can be excellent mental roadmaps for understanding. Those simple sticky concepts can remind your team why they matter and where you all are headed.

In leadership, your story is more than a side note; it's a signal.

🧠 CLARITY IN ACTION: LEAD WITH AWARENESS

Before your next tough conversation or big meeting, take 60 seconds and ask yourself:

- "What emotions are in the room?"
- "How might my words or tone land with others?"
- "What outcome do I want, and how can empathy get us there?"

Then lead with intention. Emotional intelligence builds bridges that last.

⚒ TOOLS TO CRAFT YOUR LEADERSHIP STORY

You don't need a podium, a global spotlight, or a million viewers watching your social media live-stream. All you need to use are the stories you already have that demonstrate growth, adversity, and triumph.

One of the first stories ever told was how we used to live, chickens being thrown over our heads to treat chicken pox as kids. These simple stories serve as connectors and can be excellent mental roadmaps for understanding. Those simple sticky concepts can remind your team why they matter and where you all are headed.

In leadership, your story is more than a side note; it's a signal.

Add these to your storytelling toolkit today:

- **Start with "why"** – Why does this story matter to the moment or message?
- **Use vivid detail** – What did it feel like? What did you see, hear, or experience?
- **Keep it tight** – Focus on the core conflict and the resolution
- **Practice delivery** – Use pauses, vary your tone, and make eye contact
- **End with purpose** – Make sure the takeaway is clear and actionable

🔍 CHAPTER REFLECTION: MASTERING CONNECTION THROUGH STORYTELLING

Storytelling is the human side of leadership communication. It connects logic to empathy, and insight to identity.

Reflection Questions:

- What leadership story has shaped who I am?
- When have I used a story to shift a room?
- What's a story I could tell that connects to our team's mission right now?

💡 Leadership Tool: Storytelling Framework

Use this tool when preparing talks, keynotes, team updates, or coaching sessions.

- ☑ What's the leadership challenge or moment I want to highlight?
- ☑ Who's the central character or team?
- ☑ What was the conflict or turning point?
- ☑ What was the result or transformation?
- ☑ What's the leadership principle or call to action?

🧩 CONNECTION TO THE L.E.A.D. MODEL

Storytelling strengthens every piece of the L.E.A.D. Model:

- ● It starts by **listening** to others' experiences
- ● It **empowers** by showing possibility and resilience
- ● It **adapts** to fit the moment, audience, and message
- ● It **delivers** both information *and* inspiration

When you tell the right story, at the right time, with the right purpose, your leadership sticks.

🔥 BONUS LEADERSHIP NUGGET #6: BE THE STORY, BEFORE THE STAT

People don't follow bullet points; they follow belief.

The myth is that logic leads, and emotion distracts. However, it's stories, not stats, that move people to act. You can present all the right numbers, charts, and plans, but if your message doesn't land emotionally, it won't stick.

Facts inform the mind. Stories stir the heart. Great leaders use both, but they lead with the story.

When you share a personal story, you aren't just talking, you're transferring trust. You're saying, *"I've been there. I get it. And here's what I learned."* That's what creates a connection. That's what builds belief.

So, before you speak data, speak truth.

Before you deliver the numbers, provide the meaning behind them. Because when people feel the story, they'll fight for the outcome.

Be the story before the stat.

📢 Leadership Nugget Reflection Prompts: Be the Story, Before the Stat

These prompts are designed to help you think beyond information and step into transformation. They'll help you lead not just with facts, but with meaning, heart, and human connection.

Reflection Prompts

1. What's a story I often tell, but haven't connected to a leadership message yet?

2. When was the last time I shared a personal moment to build trust or direction?

3. Do I rely too heavily on slides and stats? What could I say that people would feel?

4. What story from my team's journey deserves to be told more often?

5. What's one meeting, briefing, or talk this week where I can start with a story?

✴ Practice It Out Loud: Connect. Humanize. Move.

These steps help you take your leadership voice beyond the numbers and into what people remember, your story.

✳ *Four-Step Guide to Practicing It Out Loud:*

1. **Pick the Moment**

   Think of a meeting, presentation, or coaching conversation coming up. What's the outcome you want people to feel?

2. **Choose the Story**

   Select a short personal story (your own or your team's) that reflects resilience, clarity, or growth. Ensure it aligns with the moment.

3. **Anchor the Meaning**

   Ask yourself: What's the point? What value or lesson does this story convey? Boil it down into one powerful takeaway.

4. **Tell It, Then Tie It**

   Don't just tell the story, connect it. Use a line like:
   "That's why this matters to us."
   Or
   "That moment reminds me of what we're building here."

📖 REFLECTION JOURNAL – BUILDING TOMORROW'S LEADERSHIP HABITS

Turn today's story into tomorrow's connection

Use this space to reflect on moments when you chose to lead with emotion, story, or vulnerability. What did you share? How did others respond? What did you learn about yourself or your message?

Date	Story Shared	What Shifted in the Room/ Setting	What I Learned

🗣 UP NEXT: BUILDING CLARITY THROUGH MESSAGE DESIGN

You've sparked belief with stories, now you'll forge the signal.

In Chapter 7, you'll

- **Hone your core message,** so it cuts through noise like a laser
- **Craft a headline** that people can't help but repeat
- **Structure with the three-point rule,** so your ideas land and stick
- **Speak with surgical precision**: every word driving action, not distraction

🗝 *Stop burying brilliance in buzzwords.*

Start broadcasting leadership in high-definition clarity.

Your challenge: In your next update, will you supply another slide deck, or will you deliver a crystal-clear command that people remember long after you leave the room?

Clarity isn't just nice to have; it's your leadership **signal flare**.

Ready to light up Chapter 7?

BUILDING CLARITY THROUGH MESSAGE DESIGN

> *"If you can't explain it simply, you don't understand it well enough."*
>
> ~ Albert Einstein

THE LEADERSHIP MISCONCEPTION

One of the most common mistakes leaders make is believing that clarity comes from saying more slides, more data, more explanations, but clarity isn't about stacking words on top of words.

It's about knowing what matters most and making that message unmistakably clear.

The truth is, the more you overwhelm your team with noise, the less likely they are to take action. When people are unsure, they hesitate.

When they're flooded with information, they tune out. And when your message lacks direction, even the best ideas can stall.

Great leaders don't speak to sound smart; they speak to create movement. They know how to turn complexity into confidence, and strategy into steps people can actually take.

Clarity isn't about dumbing things down or stripping away depth. It's about making meaning accessible.

It's the difference between a map and a maze, and it's one of the most underrated leadership skills you can build.

🎯 WHY CLARITY MATTERS

In today's fast-paced, high-pressure environments, clarity is essential. Your team doesn't need a flood of data or a dozen options.

They need to know where to focus, what matters, and how they fit into the bigger picture.

- ☑ A clear message:
- ☑ Builds trust by removing guesswork
- ☑ Accelerates execution by reducing delays and confusion
- ☑ Unites teams by centering everyone around a shared goal
- ☑ Increases confidence by making priorities obvious

Think of clarity as your leadership signal. If your message is cloudy, people stall. If it's clear, they move.

Clarity is not about oversimplifying. Instead, it's about organizing complexity into actionable insights. This is why effective communication is a leadership advantage.

THE THREE PILLARS OF CLEAR MESSAGE DESIGN

One of the worst things you can do is "Winging It." The reason is messaging without design is just noise.

Here are some essential pillars of message design:

Focus – What's the most critical idea?

Structure – Organize content logically: beginning, middle, end

Simplicity – Use plain language. Avoid jargon. Edit ruthlessly.

Clarity is not talent, it's a discipline.

📊 FRAMEWORK: THE THREE-POINT RULE

Cognitive analysis consistently supports the idea that people process and remember information more easily when it is grouped into sets of three.

According to studies in cognitive psychology and communication theory, including Dr. Brian Wansink's research at Cornell University and principles popularized by communication experts like Chip Heath and Dan Heath in *Made to Stick* and Cliff Atkinson in *Beyond Bullet Points*, audiences retain and engage with content best when it's organized into triads.

Whether you're giving a briefing, a keynote, or a performance update:

- Define three core points
- Organize them logically
- Reinforce the main message at the end

This structure gives your message rhythm, retention, and repeatability, a powerful asset for leadership communication.

☑ REAL-WORLD EXAMPLE: LEADING THROUGH FIRST-TIME COMPLEXITY

During a time when I was overseeing the Department of Defense's regional disbursement operations, my team was tasked with executing a high-visibility bilateral program supporting a major Air Force initiative. It was a first-of-its-kind mission, complex, high-stakes, and under an international spotlight.

What made it more challenging? It required coordination across multiple U.S. Agencies, international diplomacy, and seamless financial execution between governments.

There was a temptation was to over-explain using endless reports and jargon. Instead of letting the massive amounts of data slow us down, I chose clarity. We created a three-part communication structure:

Clarify the mission: What are we here to accomplish, and why does it matter?

Identify accountability: Who owns what, and how will we stay aligned?

Define success: What outcomes signal we've done our job well?

We used plain language, clear visuals, and consistent touch points across departments. The clarity cut through bureaucracy and built confidence among all stakeholders, from front-line technicians to foreign dignitaries. The mission was a great success because the message was clear.

📄 HISTORICAL EXAMPLE: STEVE JOBS AND THE LAUNCH OF THE IPHONE

On January 9, 2007, the stage was set at the Macworld Conference and Expo. Steve Jobs stepped onto the stage and introduced a product that would reshape the future: the iPhone.

But what made that moment legendary wasn't just the product. It was the clarity of his message. Jobs didn't bury the audience in technical specs. Instead, he focused on three revolutionary functions:

- A widescreen iPod with touch controls
- A revolutionary mobile phone
- A breakthrough internet communicator

He repeated the trio until it became unmistakable: "An iPod, a phone, and an internet communicator... all in one device." Jobs used simplicity, suspense, and repetition to make sure the world understood the product and its innovation. That clarity successfully launched the first iPhone and a global movement.

⊘ CONNECTION ACROSS TIME: THE THREE-POINT RULE STILL WORKS

When Steve Jobs introduced the iPhone, his genius was in his clarity. He took something complex and made it accessible. His message was understood, repeated, and remembered.

In any organization, leaders face moments when they must deal with a challenge that is both big and new.

When this happens, the most effective strategy is to adopt a clear and well-designed message. One that says: here's what we're doing, why it matters, and how your part of it.

When people understand, they act. Clarity in action fuels purposeful movement.

CLARITY IN ACTION: SIMPLIFY TO AMPLIFY

Before your next team brief, ask yourself:

- "What's the ONE thing they need to know?"
- "Have I stripped away jargon and excess?"
- "Could a teammate repeat this back with confidence?"

Then deliver with focus. Because in leadership, clarity is momentum.

TOOLS FOR CLEAR MESSAGE DESIGN

- **Lead with the headline** – What's the one thing they must remember?
- **Use bullet points or visuals** – Break content into digestible pieces
- **Tell them why it matters** – Link every message to mission or values
- **Repeat the core message** – Repetition builds retention
- **Ask for feedback** – "Does this make sense?" Invites understanding

🔍 CHAPTER REFLECTION: BUILDING CLARITY THROUGH MESSAGE DESIGN

Your job as a leader isn't to just sound impressive. It's to make others confident in what you say and capable to act upon it.

Reflection Questions:

- What's the one idea I need my team to remember this week?
- How can I convey my next message effectively without compromising its substance?
- Am I using clear, direct language or hiding behind jargon?

💡 LEADERSHIP TOOL: MESSAGE DESIGN PLANNER

Use this planner before briefings, announcements, or updates to sharpen clarity and drive action.

🔍 My core message is: _____

_____

🔍 Three key points: 1) _____ 2) _____ 3) _____

_____

🔍 Analogy or example to support it: _____

_____

🔍 Why it matters to the audience: _____

_____

🔍 Delivery method (email, huddle, presentation): _____

_____

🧩 CONNECTION TO THE L.E.A.D. MODEL

Strong message design strengthens every part of your leadership:

- You listen better when your team knows what to say
- You empower others when expectations are clear
- You adapt your message for different contexts and audiences
- You deliver decisions that stick and drive momentum

When you lead with clarity, you lead with confidence, and your team follows with trust.

🔊 BONUS LEADERSHIP NUGGET #7: SAY LESS. MEAN MORE.

MYTH: The loudest person in the room is leading the room. If you flood the air with wisdom, stack up the talking points, and fill every gap, everyone will know you're in charge.

TRUTH: That's what I thought at first, too. I figured if I had the mic, I'd better use every second. More words, more power, right?

Wrong. The leaders people remember are the ones who can make a room pause, with one phrase that make them sit up straighter, that didn't try to fill the space but landed with real weight.

Let me tell you: Early on, I was the king of the meeting monologue. I'd lay it all out, hunting for impact in the details. I'd see my team glaze over and blame them for missing the message, when the truth was, the message was buried under a pile of extra words. When you overload, you don't impress; you get ignored.

Reality check? In a world drowning in noise, nobody's got time to dig through your chapter to find the headline. The leaders who matter know when to let their words breathe, let silence work, let the one sentence that matters do its job.

The best lines don't just fill up time. They leave an echo. They stick with you after everyone shuts their laptops. Sometimes the most powerful leader in the room is the one who lets their pause do the heavy lifting, who cuts straight to what matters, and then stops, because what's said is enough.

So next time you feel the itch to explain, to go on one more tangent, to wrap every thought in a long-winded story, do this: Bite your tongue. Rethink that paragraph. Sharpen it to a sentence that can't be forgotten.

You don't lead by talking more. You lead by making your words stick.

Say less. Mean more. Make people feel it when you speak, and even more when you don't. Because sometimes the loudest thing you can do... is let your meaning ring out in the quiet.

📢 Leadership Nugget Reflection Prompts: Say Less. Mean More.

These prompts are designed to help you evaluate how you communicate, not just what you say, but how clearly, courageously, and concisely you say it. The best leaders aren't loud, they're laser focused. They don't flood rooms with words; they fill them with meaning.

Reflection Prompts

1. When I speak, do people leave with clarity or just content?

2. Where do I tend to over-explain? What's driving that?

3. What is a recent moment where fewer words could've made more impact?

4. Do I check for understanding, or assume it?

5. What is one message I need to sharpen this week?

6. How often do I use silence, questions, or repetition to reinforce clarity?

Practice It Out Loud: Clarity Is a Leadership Skill

Use this four-step guide to simplify your message, amplify your impact, and establish a reputation for clear and confident communication.

✳ *Four-Step Guide to Practicing It Out Loud:*

1. **Spot the Noise**

   What message or topic are you over-complicating right now?
   Identify where the message is getting lost in too much explanation.

2. **Sharpen the Signal**

   What's the one thing you want your audience to walk away with?
   Say it in 10 words or less. Write it. Repeat it. Own it.

3. **Choose the Strongest Frame**

   Turn your message into a story, visual, or repeatable phrase. Simplified doesn't mean shallow, it means sticky.

4. **Check for Echo, Not Applause**

   After you speak, listen for the echo.
   Did they get it? Can they repeat it? If not, refine, not rewind.

📓 REFLECTION JOURNAL — BUILDING TOMORROW'S LEADERSHIP HABITS

Turn today's words into tomorrow's impact

Use this space to reflect on how your clarity shaped momentum. Where did your words unlock movement, change a mindset, or eliminate confusion?

What did you say less of, and mean more with?

Date	Message/Topic	What You Simplified	Outcome/What Shifted

🗣 UP NEXT: DEVELOPING CONNECTION THROUGH EMOTIONAL INTELLIGENCE

You've mastered clarity, now it's time to feel the room.

In Chapter 8, you'll

- **Tune into unspoken signals** so you spot tension before it blows up
- **Name what matters** by translating emotion into strategic action
- **Hold the space** so people feel seen, heard, and safe to speak up
- **Navigate with empathy,** turning conflict into collaboration

🔑 *Pause to pontificate and you risk missing the real message.*

Lean into emotion, and you unlock deeper trust and loyalty.

Your challenge: In your next interaction, will you just deliver information, or will you lead with empathy and watch your influence grow?

Emotional intelligence isn't a soft skill; it's your leadership **radar**. Ready to tune in for Chapter 8?

DEVELOPING CONNECTION THROUGH EMOTIONAL INTELLIGENCE

> *"When dealing with people, remember you are not dealing with creatures of logic, but creatures of emotion."*
>
> ~ Dale Carnegie

🔍 THE LEADERSHIP MISCONCEPTION

A common misconception is that leadership and emotion don't belong in the same room. Many still believe that great leaders rely solely on logic and leave their emotions at the door. Consequently, that mindset ignores the critical fact that humans aren't machines. We don't make decisions in a vacuum. We bring emotion, context, and lived experience to almost every decision.

To ignore emotion is to ignore reality. You can have a foolproof plan, a brilliant strategy, and the clearest communication, but if you cannot gauge the emotional temperature of your team, you'll miss the mark as a leader.

Emotional intelligence isn't a soft skill; it's a strategic one. It's the difference between managing people and truly leading them.

💡 WHAT IS EMOTIONAL INTELLIGENCE?

Emotional Intelligence (EI) is defined as the ability to recognize, understand, and manage your own emotions and the emotions of others.

High-EI leaders foster stronger connections, diffuse conflict more effectively, build trust faster, and create environments where people feel psychologically safe to perform at their best.

The Four Pillars of Emotional Intelligence

The leaders we remember aren't just the smartest in the room; they're the ones who can read it, feel it, and steer it without losing themselves in the process.

They master the moment, and the moment doesn't master them. They know when to push, when to pause, and they know how to see emotion and not lead with it.

That's emotional intelligence. **It's not a "soft skill**, but it is a hard one because if you can't handle your own emotions, you are guaranteed to have a hard time leading anyone.

However, there are four pillars, which are the four cornerstones of emotional intelligence. When built strong, it lets you stand steady no matter how rough the winds get.

1. **Self-awareness** – Recognizing your emotions and their impact

2. **Self-management** – Staying calm, adaptable, and composed under stress

3. **Social awareness** – Reading the room and picking up on nonverbal cues

4. **Relationship management** – Communicating with empathy, inspiring others, and resolving conflict

These four elements are what turn good communicators into transformational leaders.

☑ REAL-WORLD EXAMPLE: LEADING WITH EMPATHY

When I served as Chairman of the International Cooperative Administrative Support Services (ICASS) Council at the U.S. Embassy, I was responsible for managing the embassy's multi-million-dollar operating budget.

In this role, I coordinated with over 50 government, federal, and non-governmental agencies.

The mission was dynamic and fast-paced. Resources were limited but highly competitive. Desired objectives were subjective, based on who was asking the question. Departments had organizational objectives that they had to fiercely protect. In short, emotions often ran high.

I decided that instead of asserting control or forcing compliance, I would choose a different path: emotional intelligence.

First, I committed to keeping my emotions in check as I listened, empathized, and validated the emotions of my team members.

I met personally with each key stakeholder, learning about their positions and re-framing their problems as shared challenges. I spoke about purpose, not pressure, and how we needed their input to reach a shared vision.

What could've become chaos turned into collaboration. Teams aligned. Energy returned, and progress accelerated.

Emotional intelligence didn't dilute the leadership, it amplified it.

📄 HISTORICAL EXAMPLE: SATYA NADELLA AND THE CULTURE SHIFT AT MICROSOFT

When Satya Nadella became CEO of Microsoft in 2014, the company was struggling with internal silos, stagnation, and a reputation for rigidity.

Nadella didn't start with technical overhauls. He didn't walk in with anger and frustration, even though those emotions, among many others, were present. He took a different approach, and that was to lead with empathy.

Nadella introduced a culture rooted in emotional intelligence, where listening mattered, failure was viewed as a learning tool, and collaboration was valued over competition.

His signature phrase was "Hit refresh," and this wasn't just a tech metaphor.

Under Nadella's emotionally intelligent leadership, Microsoft's market value tripled.

More importantly, its culture transformed, proving that empathy is a competitive advantage.

⨂ CONNECTION ACROSS TIME: EMOTIONAL INTELLIGENCE = CONNECTIVITY

When Satya Nadella reshaped Microsoft's culture, he didn't lead with dominance, he led with emotional insight. That insight evolved into higher morale, deeper trust, and stronger performance.

Emotional intelligence isn't reserved for CEOs or diplomatic councils; it's a tool that every leader can utilize.

When people feel seen, they show up. When they feel heard, they engage, and when they feel respected, they rise.

In any workplace, team room, or boardroom, emotional intelligence is the connective tissue between clarity and trust.

⨂ CLARITY IN ACTION: EMOTIONAL INTELLIGENCE ON DISPLAY

When leaders show emotional intelligence, it is not a sign of sensitivity or weakness. Rather, it's about leading with clarity *and* compassion. It means knowing when to speak and when to listen. When to push and when to pause. When to hold the line and when to hold space.

Emotionally intelligent leaders do three things well:

- **They notice** what others miss: tone, tension, timing.
- **They name** what's unspoken: fear, frustration, fatigue.

- **They navigate** with empathy, adjusting their style but not their standards.

Emotional intelligence isn't softness. It's strategic clarity. Because people follow leaders who understand them.

🛠️ TOOLS TO LEAD WITH EMOTIONAL INTELLIGENCE

- **Pause before responding** – Take a breath. Let the emotion settle before the decision.
- **Name the emotion** – "It sounds like this is really frustrating." Acknowledgment builds trust.
- **Ask before you assume** – "How are you doing with this change?" Opens a real conversation.
- **Reframe conflict as collaboration** – Shift from "us vs. them" to "we're solving this together."
- **Stay steady in emotionally charged moments** – Your calm can reset the room.

These small habits create psychological safety. They show your team they're seen, heard, and valued, even when the mission is tough.

🔍 CHAPTER REFLECTION: DEVELOPING CONNECTION THROUGH EMOTIONAL INTELLIGENCE

Being emotionally intelligent doesn't mean being emotional. It means being attuned to yourself and to others. It's the difference between communication that checks a box and communication that changes behavior.

Reflection Questions:

- Do I recognize my emotional triggers before I act?
- How well do I respond when others are frustrated or overwhelmed?
- When was the last time I led with empathy, versus only direction?
- What does it feel like to be led by me?

💡 LEADERSHIP TOOL: EMOTIONAL INTELLIGENCE DAILY CHECK-IN

Emotions change like the weather, and sometimes things can be a beautiful sunny (happy) day, and the next thing you know, it's a full storm (anger, frustration, etc.).

It's due to this probability that you must check in with your emotional awareness daily.

Use this check-in as part of your daily prep or end-of-day reflection.

- ☑ What am I feeling right now?
- ☑ What might my team be feeling?
- ☑ Did I ask someone how they're doing and listen fully to their response?
- ☑ Did I pause before reacting?
- ☑ Did I offer empathy or just instruction?

Remember, emotional intelligence is like a muscle; the more you use it, the stronger it gets.

✿ CONNECTION TO THE L.E.A.D. MODEL

Emotional intelligence strengthens every piece of the L.E.A.D. Model:

- You **Listen** with empathy and understanding
- You **Empower** through psychological safety
- You **Adapt** by sensing emotional shifts and responding well
- You **Deliver** decisions that reflect emotional awareness

To lead out loud is to lead with both clarity and compassion.

BONUS LEADERSHIP NUGGET #8: STOIC ≠ STRONG

MYTH: Strong leaders hide their emotions, show no cracks, and wear a mask of toughness. To be stoic is a strength.

TRUTH: Real power comes from presence, not silence. When you shut down, you disconnect. When you show up real and authentic, you begin to lead with true strength.

Here's where most leaders go wrong: They were taught to "lead like nothing's wrong," to hide every feeling and tough it out alone, but stuffing emotions doesn't armor you; it isolates you. Silence isn't strength, it's distance. Every unspoken worry, every hidden doubt, adds a brick to the wall between you and your team.

Somewhere along the way, we confused being steady with being stoic, but true strength isn't about shutting down; it's about tuning in. Emotional intelligence isn't chaos, it's context. It's the compass that helps you read the room, notice the struggling employee, name the unspoken, and respond with clarity and purpose. It doesn't make you fragile; it makes you effective. It doesn't make you soft; it makes you strategic.

Great leaders don't hide above the surface or behind a poker face; they show up honest, grounded, and unafraid to lead with empathy as their advantage. Empathy doesn't weaken leadership; it deepens it. So next time you catch yourself clamming up, remember: Presence beats stoicism every time.

Name what you feel before it names you.

Share the why behind your calm. **Trust your honesty more than your armor.**

Stop bottling up. Lean in. Stoic ≠ strong. Present = powerful.

Don't just lead loud enough to be heard, lead real enough to be felt. That's what breaks down the fortress, turns distance into trust, and shows your team what courage looks like.

▨ Leadership Nugget Reflection Prompts: Stoic ≠ Strong

These prompts help you reflect on emotional intelligence, not as a buzzword, but as a leadership advantage rooted in awareness, empathy, and presence.

Reflection Prompts

1. When was the last time I led through emotion, not around it?

2. Do I give my team permission to express their feelings, or do I model silence?

3. What emotion have I been ignoring that might carry a message?

4. How would my leadership shift if I saw emotion as a signal, not a weakness?

5. Do I model emotional awareness or emotional avoidance?

6. What's one area I need to lead with margin, not just motion, this week?

✷ Practice It Out Loud: Leading with Steady Emotion.

Emotional intelligence is more than knowing how you feel. It's using that insight to lead with strength and connection, without collapsing under pressure.

✳ *Four-Step Guide to Practicing It Out Loud:*

1. **Tune In, Don't Turn Off**

   Take one moment today to pause and check your emotional temperature. Are you aware, or just avoiding?

2. **Swap Silence for Signal**

   In your next team meeting or check-in, offer one sentence that signals presence, not perfection.
   Ex: "I know this is a tough week. I'm here to support where I can."

3. **Name the Emotion, Not Just the Task**

   When leading through conflict or stress, call out what's felt, not just what's expected.
   Ex: "I sense there's some hesitation here, what's on your mind?"

4. **Model Emotional Margin**

   Show your team that calm isn't passive, it's powerful. Practice one moment today where you model control without being cold.

📓 REFLECTION JOURNAL – LEADING WITH PRESENCE, NOT PRETENSE

Turn today's awareness into tomorrow's leadership advantage

Use this space to reflect on moments when you chose to tune in, not shut down.

What did you notice in the room, or in yourself?

How did leading with emotional intelligence shift the outcome?

Date	Moment	How I Showed Up with Presence	What Shifted/ Improved

🗣 UP NEXT: INSPIRING ACTION THROUGH VISION AND PURPOSE

You've tuned into the human side, now you get to cast the big picture.

In Chapter 9, you'll

- **Paint the horizon** so every role feels part of something greater
- **Link today's tasks** to tomorrow's purpose to ignite genuine buy-in
- **Speak in "We" not "I"** to build shared ownership and momentum
- **Turn aspirations into action** with clear milestones and celebration points

🔑 *Stay stuck in logistics, and your team becomes cogs.*

Lead with vision, and they become champions of your mission.

Your challenge: In your next team huddle, will you detail the "what" or will you unveil the "why" that people rally around?

Vision isn't a poster on the wall; it's your leadership **north star**.

Ready to light the way in Chapter 9?

PART III

BUILD A LEGACY

Inspiring Action Through Vision and Purpose

Sustaining Leadership Energy and Resilience

Final Reflections and Leading Your Legacy

INSPIRING ACTION THROUGH VISION AND PURPOSE

> *"Leadership is the capacity to translate vision into reality."*
>
> ~ *Warren Bennis*

 THE LEADERSHIP MISCONCEPTION

Vision is often mistaken for a mission statement (you know that poster pinned to the wall in the break room), but they are very different indeed.

Vision connects the tasks at hand to a greater purpose. It moves people. It inspires.

The goal of purpose-driven leadership isn't to get people to work harder, it is to give them a reason to care, and then to clear a path to action.

Strategy gets you to the destination and vision tells you why the destination matters.

WHY VISION MATTERS

Vision gives your team a destination. Purpose gives them the reason to go.

When leaders cast a clear, compelling vision:

- People align around shared outcomes
- Silos begin to dissolve
- Commitment replaces compliance
- Innovation grows from belief, not obligation

Without vision, even talented teams burn out. With vision, ordinary teams achieve the extraordinary.

🗝 Components of a Powerful Vision

- **Clarity** – What exactly are we working toward?
- **Relevance** – How does it connect to our values and mission?
- **Inspiration** – Why should it matter emotionally or ethically?
- **Actionability** – What can each person do to help get us there?

Great visions are felt, not just understood.

☑ REAL-WORLD EXAMPLE: "FIGHT TONIGHT" A MISSION WITH MEANING

In November 2014, I was stationed on a military installation in South Korea where I was beginning a 12-month short tour. Our installation was only a few hundred miles from one of the world's most volatile borders.

The hard truth was that if a missile or chemical attack were launched, we would have roughly ten minutes from detection to impact. Ten minutes to act. Ten minutes to call the ones we loved. Ten minutes to prepare for the unthinkable.

A few days after arriving, we were all gathered in a large theater awaiting an address by the Wing Commander. I was surrounded by fellow Airmen, my adrenaline high and nerves quietly buzzing.

We all stood at attention as the Wing Commander entered, a Colonel, sharp, composed, and commanding in presence. He wasted no time in addressing his troops.

"Our job here is simple," he said. "We're here to Fight Tonight. Not tomorrow. Not after lunch. Tonight."

He didn't give us slogans. He gave us purpose. He spoke of readiness, deterrence, and our role in shaping global stability. He made it clear that our preparation wasn't just strategic, it was a message to the world that, if challenged, we would respond with precision and strength.

Whatever fear or anxiety was in that room evaporated with every deliberately chosen word. The mental fatigue of the "ten minutes" faded. We weren't just deployed. We were empowered. We were part of a mission larger than ourselves.

When people know their purpose and believe in it, they don't hesitate. They move.

That moment motivated and aligned the entire theatre. His words allowed us to bond and be ready to lead with clarity, courage, and conviction.

📑 HISTORICAL EXAMPLE: ADMIRAL MICHELLE HOWARD AND VISIONARY ACTION

When Admiral Michelle Howard became the first woman to achieve the rank of four-star admiral in the U.S. Navy, and the first African American woman to command a U.S. Navy ship, she was tasked with leading through uncertainty, crisis, and international complexity.

In one of her most high-profile moments, she led operations during the 2009 Maersk Alabama hijacking, when Somali pirates held Captain Richard Phillips hostage.

Howard didn't panic and didn't posture. Instead, she focused her team on the following clear and courageous vision: preserve life, protect sovereignty, and resolve the crisis with discipline.

Her leadership was decisive, composed, and rooted in purpose. That clarity mobilized a successful operation and saved lives under unimaginable pressure.

◎ CONNECTION ACROSS TIME: CLEAR VISION MOVES PEOPLE

When Admiral Michelle Howard led her team through a high-stakes hostage crisis, she relied on tactical skill combined with clarity of mission and purpose.

Her ability to calmly and confidently unify her team behind that vision turned a potential disaster into a model of modern military leadership.

But this isn't just about military leaders.

Any leader, in any industry, can inspire extraordinary performance through a compelling vision.

Whether you're leading a business transformation, managing a school district, or launching a community initiative, when people understand why they matter, they give more than just their labor. They give their belief.

Vision is about moving people from pressure to purpose, and from uncertainty to unity.

✏️ CLARITY IN ACTION: PUTTING VISION TO WORK

Vision becomes more powerful when it's stated and then activated. Here's how leaders can translate inspiration into execution:

- **Make it tangible** – Break down the vision into specific, actionable milestones.
- **Connect the dots** – Regularly link team efforts to the larger purpose.
- **Repeat with passion** – Communicate the vision consistently with emotion and authenticity.
- **Celebrate alignment** – Recognize when actions align with the vision to reinforce desired behaviors.
- **Course-correct with purpose** – When the path shifts, reframe the challenge in the context of the bigger mission.

Clarity in vision leads to clarity in action. And when people know where they're going, and why, they'll bring more than effort. They'll bring belief.

🛠️ TOOLS TO INSPIRE THROUGH VISION

- **Paint the picture** – Use vivid, emotional language
- **Tell the story** – Make it relatable and values-based
- **Use "we" language** – Create shared identity and ownership
- **Set milestones** – Break the vision into meaningful wins
- **Celebrate progress** – Reinforce belief through momentum

🔍 CHAPTER REFLECTION: INSPIRING ACTION THROUGH VISION

Your team needs goals, but they also need to know that what they're doing matters. A leader's voice should direct and ignite.

Reflection Questions:

- What is the vision I want my team to rally around?
- Is that vision clear, meaningful, and actionable?
- How often do I connect today's work to tomorrow's purpose?
- Do my people feel inspired or just informed?

🔆 LEADERSHIP TOOL: VISION & PURPOSE CANVAS

Use this with your team to translate vision into shared direction.

- ✅ Our Vision: _____
- ✅ Why It Matters: _____
- ✅ Who It Serves: _____
- ✅ What Success Looks Like: _____
- ✅ Key Milestones: _____
- ✅ My Next Step as a Leader: _____

🍀 CONNECTION TO THE L.E.A.D. MODEL

Vision brings your L.E.A.D. Foundation to life:

- You **listen** to uncover values and needs
- You **empower** people to own their part in the vision
- You **adapt** messaging as challenges evolve
- You **deliver** a message that inspires and sustains action

To lead out loud is to help people believe in something bigger than themselves, and then to act on it.

BONUS LEADERSHIP NUGGET #9: CAST FIRE, NOT FOG

Can Your Vision Pass the Fire Test?

MYTH: Vision lives on pretty posters and a killer mission statement. Make it shiny, make it clever, hang it in the hallway, that's how you get people on board.

TRUTH: Here's what nobody brags about at those rah-rah off-sites: Real vision doesn't hang on a wall; it burns right through you. **If your mission can't light up the cynic in the back row, or survive your next Monday meltdown, it's just another fog machine.** Fog not only restricts vision clarity, but it also stifles the spark and leaves your team cold, wondering who will ever light the match.

I've watched more than one leader fall for the trap: obsessing over sound bites and branding, thinking conviction is just a snazzy tagline. Funny thing, most of those taglines end up forgotten, buried under next year's slogan. The teams that build something are not quoting a laminated poster. They're fired up from something so simple and straightforward even a 12-year-old could explain it, and so alive your harshest critic would fight for it on their worst day.

Here's the real gut check: can your vision pass the Fire Test?

- ☑ Could your 12-year-old nephew explain it back to you?
- ☑ Would the skeptic in the room offer to help, even if there was no paycheck?
- ☑ Does your vision hold when you're tired, your patience is shot, and nobody's clapping?

If you can't say "hell yes" to all three, you're still living in the fog. I know we've seen fog so often that we think fog looks strategic. We can be so convinced of its strategy, right up until your team is lost in it, then we notice logs stacked, waiting for someone brave enough to take the reins and megaphone to lead the way.

Your people don't need another "statement." They need that moment when they lock eyes and quietly say: "I'm in. Let's go." That's when you know you've cast fire, and fire is honest. One ember is all it takes to turn a slow morning into a wildfire.

So, strip away the clever branded sound bites. Speak like it matters (because it does). Name what's really at stake, even if it's scary. Paint the target so clearly it burns a hole in the excuses and anchor it in a "why" they can feel, not just memorize.

Cloudy goals have never moved anyone, but I've seen folks run through brick walls for a vision that burned hot enough to pull them in.

Don't baby the thermostat. Vision isn't about "keeping it comfortable." It's the torch you hand over at the start of the race and hope your team runs with after you're long gone. The goal isn't to be heard, it's to set something on fire that keeps burning after every meeting's over and the applause dies out.

So, light the flame. Get uncomfortable. Make the vision so real that they can feel the heat from across the room.

Cast fire, not fog, because nobody gets moving for something they can barely see; they run for what sets them ablaze.

Leadership Nugget Reflection Prompts: Cast Fire, Not Fog

These prompts help you test whether your vision is sparking belief or clouding the room with vagueness.

Great leaders don't whisper safe hopes; they ignite shared conviction. Use these questions to lead with heat and clarity.

Reflection Prompts

1. Where have I hidden behind safe language instead of striking a bold spark?

2. What part of our vision feels crystal clear to me but remains foggy for my team?

3. Which buzzwords have I repeated that need replacing with vivid "what if" scenarios?

4. When was the last time my words lit a fire, versus just warming the room?

5. What concrete example or story can I use next to turn hesitation into momentum?

6. In my next team touchpoint, where will I cast the torch of vision instead of cranking the thermostat?

Practice It Out Loud: Speak the Spark. Lead the Flame.

These moves help you turn vision into fuel, not just fancy phrasing.

Leadership isn't about sounding smart. It's about being seen, felt, and followed.

✳ Four-Step Guide to Practicing It Out Loud:

1. **Identify the Fog Zone**

   Where are you losing clarity in your vision?
   Is it a project, a person, or your own internal messaging?

2. **Name the Flame**

   What core belief fuels this vision?
   If you stripped away every slide and stat, what message would remain?

3. **Test the Transfer**

   Does your message pass the clarity test?
   Ask one teammate: "What do you think this means, and why does it matter?"

4. **Fuel the Fire Weekly**

   Vision fades if it's not refueled.
   Where, in your next team huddle, email, or one-on-one meeting, can you restate the vision *clearly and courageously*?

📖 REFLECTION JOURNAL – SPEAK WHAT YOU SEE, FUEL WHAT YOU BELIEVE

Track where your clarity creates momentum

Use this space to record the moments when your words moved people from confusion to conviction.

Where did you replace fog with fire? What reactions did you notice? What message lit a spark?

Date	Foggy Area or Confused Outcome	Message Re-framed	What Sparked/ Shifted

 UP NEXT: SUSTAINING LEADERSHIP ENERGY AND RESILIENCE

You've galvanized belief with vision, now it's time to keep the flame burning.

In Chapter 10, you'll

- **Spot the burn zones** before they become burnout crises
- **Anchor with rituals** that recharge you, not just refuel the day
- **Set boundaries boldly** so your fire doesn't fizzle into frenzy
- **Model recovery** so your team learns to sustain, not just survive

🔑 *Push nonstop, and you spark burnout.*

Lead with intention, and you become the lighthouse everyone steers toward.

Your challenge: In your next week, will you sprint until you stop, or will you build the steady fire that outlasts every storm?

Endurance isn't about raw stamina; it's your leadership **lighthouse**.

Ready to keep the flame alive in Chapter 10?

SUSTAINING LEADERSHIP ENERGY AND RESILIENCE

> *"Resilience is knowing that you are the only one who has the power and the responsibility to pick yourself up."*
>
> ~ Mary Holloway

THE LEADERSHIP MISCONCEPTION

There's a persistent myth that strong leaders are always go-go-go, never slowing down, grinding nonstop, and showing up no matter what. Let me be the first to tell you, that belief is truly dangerous.

Leadership isn't about endless hustle. Instead, it's about focused sustainability. The truth is that burnout doesn't build trust, and exhaustion doesn't lead to inspired teams. Running on empty signals imbalance, and this is not how you model strength.

Resilient leaders know that their energy is not unlimited. They protect it, recharge it, and lead from a place of wholeness, not depletion. The best leaders don't just show up once, they show up consistently.

⚡ WHY ENERGY AND RESILIENCE MATTER

Leadership is a marathon, not a sprint. It demands stamina, focus, and emotional discipline.

Every day brings pressures, deadlines, setbacks, and curveballs that can drain even the most seasoned leaders. When energy starts fading, so does your ability to lead with clarity, confidence, precision and compassion.

This is why resilience is more than just a personal strength; it's a leadership necessity. Sustaining your energy and mental bandwidth is a strategy versus a sign of weakness. A leader who is energized and grounded is far more capable of supporting, guiding, and inspiring others through any challenge.

☑ REAL-WORLD EXAMPLE: BOUNDARIES, BURNOUT, AND THE COVID WAKE-UP CALL

In May 2020, during the height of the COVID pandemic, our organization, like most others around the world, transitioned to a telework schedule. At first, I welcomed the change. I was working from home, in my pajamas, with what seemed like unlimited time to accomplish my daily tasks. Not having to commute was also a pleasure, and having all my favorite snacks within arm's reach was an added bonus. The first week felt like a dream.

But by week two, my energy began to shift. I didn't have a schedule. I answered emails at all hours. **Some days I worked up to 16 hours straight.** As the days blurred together, I could feel my energy and focus fading. I was losing my capacity to connect with my team members which meant my ability to lead with clarity, confidence, and compassion was also fading. I was slowly burning out.

That's when my wife pulled me aside and asked, "Are you okay?"

Interestingly, when your sustainable energy is fading, others often notice it before you do. This is why it's critical to have trusted people around you who will give you honest feedback.

At that moment, I knew I had to make some changes.

We converted one of our rooms into an office. **I set clear boundaries, including start and end times, a consistent lunch break, and a strict end-of-day cutoff.** After those boundaries were established, my energy soared, which in turn boosted my connection with my team and increased my mental availability for them.

During our weekly staff meeting, I shared what I had learned and how my energy had been compromised. That honest reflection led several others to make changes as well. Sustainable leadership supports you while also setting the tone for everyone you lead.

🕰 HISTORICAL EXAMPLE: JACINDA ARDERN'S RESILIENT LEADERSHIP DURING CRISIS

In 2020, New Zealand's Prime Minister, Jacinda Ardern, became an international symbol of empathetic and steady leadership during the COVID crisis. While many world leaders delivered complex, often overwhelming updates, **Ardern stood out for her clarity, composure, and connection with the public.**

Her daily briefings were straightforward yet human. She addressed the nation in clear, concise language, acknowledged the nation's fears, and conveyed a message of hope. Ardern even went live from her home in a hoodie to talk directly with citizens, showing that vulnerability and authority could coexist.

The result? New Zealand had some of the most effective and coordinated COVID responses among the world's nations. While her leadership helped promote health policy, it also conveyed energy, tone, and trust. She modeled how sustainable leadership draws strength from consistency and connection.

⊘ CONNECTION ACROSS TIME: YOU CANNOT POUR FROM AN EMPTY CUP

Whether it's a global pandemic or a high-stakes organizational pivot, leaders are expected to show up. However, showing up consistently with focus and care requires energy that doesn't come from adrenaline; it comes from rhythm, rest, and reflection.

The lesson Jacinda Ardern reinforced is that leadership energy must be intentional. You cannot pour from an empty cup. Your capacity to lead others is directly tied to your capacity to sustain yourself.

Today's leaders can foster sustainability by incorporating rest into their routines, promoting mental wellness among their teams, and recognizing the warning signs of burnout before they become breaking points.

⚷ TOOLS TO BUILD ENERGY AND RESILIENCE

- **Routine self-check-ins** – Take 5 minutes daily to assess your energy, focus, and emotions.
- **Set boundaries** – Schedule personal time as firmly as meetings.
- **Practice mindfulness** – Use breathing techniques or short meditations to reset.
- **Seek mentorship and peer support** – Don't carry it alone.
- **Celebrate small wins** – Reinforce progress to maintain high morale.

🔍 CHAPTER REFLECTION: SUSTAINING LEADERSHIP ENERGY

Leadership isn't about pushing endlessly. It's about knowing when to recharge, how to reset, and who to lean on.

Resilience isn't resistance, it's recovery.

Reflection Questions:

- How do I manage my energy during difficult times?
- What daily or weekly habits help me recharge?
- How do I model sustainable leadership for my team?
- Who supports me, and who do I help?

💡 LEADERSHIP TOOL: ENERGY & RESILIENCE TRACKER

Energy is like breathing; you don't notice you're out of it until you're already tired. That's why it's essential to check in with yourself regularly. Use these prompts daily or weekly to track your energy and well-being:

- ☑ Hours of sleep last night: _____
- ☑ One thing that energized me today: _____
- ☑ My current stress level (1–10): _____
- ☑ What helped me recover today: _____
- ☑ Who did I connect with for support? _____
- ☑ What small win can I celebrate? _____

🧠 CLARITY IN ACTION: ENERGY AS A LEADERSHIP ASSET

Before you power through another late night or say yes to one more commitment, ask yourself:

- "Will this fuel me or drain me?"
- "What's one boundary I can reinforce to protect my energy?"
- "Am I setting an example of sustainability for those around me?"

Then lead with intention.

Because sustainable energy doesn't just serve you, it multiplies your impact.

🧩 CONNECTION TO THE L.E.A.D. MODEL

Sustainable leadership depends on:

- **Listening** to your own needs and limits
- **Empowering** yourself and others through positive energy
- **Adapting** with resilience
- **Delivering** steady leadership over time

To lead out loud means to lead with conviction and perseverance.

🔥 BONUS LEADERSHIP NUGGET #10: BURN STEADY, NOT OUT

Sustainability is the new superpower.

MYTH: Real leaders never stop. They live on caffeine and chaos, wear exhaustion like a trophy, and push until there's nothing left. First in, last out. If you're not wrecked, you're not really leading.

TRUTH: I used to buy into all of that. I thought being always-on meant I was setting the example. For years, I skipped dinners, poured another cup, hit send at 2 a.m., and called it commitment. I figured if my tank was empty, I was "all in." What I didn't see then is that burning myself down didn't lead anyone anywhere; I just smothered the room and left my team in the glow of a wick that didn't last.

Here's what you won't hear in the hustle speeches: after a while, nobody pats you on the back for being dead on your feet. They stop asking, start wondering if you'll let anyone else share the work… or if you even know how.

No one remembers who powered through the most weekends or skipped the most birthdays; they remember who was steady when things got rough, and whether anyone else could step up when you needed rest. I learned the hard way: sprinting alone isn't leadership it's running from fear or from trusting others.

The people who show up for their people, rain or shine, are the ones you follow through storms, because they last.

Your job isn't to run till you collapse or impress with all-nighters nobody asked you for; it's to set a pace that lets the whole team breathe and grow. It's owning your energy and giving others permission to own theirs.

Take it from experience: That inbox can wait. The hero act gets old fast. What sticks is showing your team how to work and live in a way that survives the long haul. Calm isn't a luxury; it's the torch they watch when everything else is rattling.

Here's what I wish I'd figured out a decade sooner: Pass work down. Go home before you're fried. Say yes to real life, not just work life. Because the real glow comes from knowing you're still burning bright when your team needs you, tonight, next week, and for every storm ahead.

Be the lighthouse, not the flare. Flares impress and vanish; lighthouses endure and guide. When your light holds, ships don't wreck; they find their way home.

Burn steady, not out. That's how you light the way without losing yourself or your crew in the process.

📣 Leadership Nugget Reflection Prompts: Burn Steady, Not Out

These prompts are designed to help you evaluate how you communicate, not just what you say, but how clearly, courageously, and concisely you say it.

The best leaders aren't loud, they're laser focused. **They don't flood rooms with words; they fill them with meaning.**

Reflection Prompts

1. Where am I showing up with fire, but not fuel?

2. When was the last time I paused, not because I crashed, but because I chose to protect my presence?

3. What patterns or people drain me faster than I can recover, and how can I replenish my energy?

4. What rituals or routines keep me grounded and focused under pressure?

5. Do I model sustainable leadership, or do I accidentally glorify burnout?

6. What's one area I need to lead with margin, not just motion, this week?

Practice It Out Loud: Burn Steady. Lead Long.

These moves help you build stamina without sacrifice. Leadership isn't about pushing harder; it's about leading wiser.

✳ *Four-Step Guide to Practicing It Out Loud:*

1. **Spot the Burn Zone**

   What areas of your leadership feel hot but unsustainable? Is it in your time, your team, your pace, or your expectations?

2. **Name Your Anchor Routine**

   What's one non-negotiable habit that grounds you, daily or weekly?
   Whether it's 15 minutes of reflection, movement, or silence, own it.

3. **Communicate Your Boundaries with Purpose**

   Boundaries aren't barriers, they're leadership clarity. What's one boundary you need to communicate to model healthy leadership for your team?

4. **Build In Recovery, Not Just Response**

   Don't wait until the crash. What's your reset plan this week? "In my next [check-in, calendar review, or planning session], I'll block space to restore, not just to react."

📖 REFLECTION JOURNAL – BUILDING TOMORROW'S LEADERSHIP HABITS

Turn today's margin into tomorrow's momentum

Use this space to capture the moments where you chose to lead from purpose, not pressure.
Where did you choose presence over performance?
What rhythms, pauses, or changes helped you sustain, not just start, your leadership energy?

Date	Situation or Pattern	Reset or Anchor Used	What Shifted or Improved

🗣 UP NEXT: FINAL REFLECTIONS AND LEADING YOUR LEGACY

Leadership is what you do *and* what you leave behind.

In the final chapter, we'll reflect on legacy, intentional influence, and how to lead out loud every day. You've stoked the steady flame, now it's **time to plant the oaks.**

In Chapter 11, you'll

- **Define your leadership imprint** so every word and action echoes beyond today
- **Invest in others** to multiply influence through mentorship and coaching
- **Build processes that endure** so your team thrives long after you move on
- **Celebrate collective impact** so legacy becomes a living, breathing culture

🔑 *Lead for the moment, and you may be forgotten. Lead for the long haul, and you become the foundation everyone builds upon.*

Your challenge: Which will you choose: a fleeting spotlight, or the deep roots that outlast storms?

Legacy isn't a footprint in the sand; it's your leadership **oak grove.**

Ready to sow seeds in Chapter 11?

FINAL REFLECTIONS AND LEADING YOUR LEGACY

> *"The greatest leader is not necessarily the one who does the greatest things. He is the one that gets the people to do the greatest things."*
>
> ~ *Ronald Reagan*

WHY LEGACY MATTERS

Leadership is more than what you accomplish, it's about what you leave behind. It's the imprint you make on others, the culture you help build, and the momentum you create that continues beyond your tenure.

Legacy isn't reserved for the end of your career. It's built into daily conversations, decisions, and interactions. Leading with legacy means leading with purpose, clarity, and conviction, always keeping your long-term impact in mind.

PRINCIPLES FOR LEADING YOUR LEGACY

- **Be intentional**: Lead with a strong sense of purpose and values.
- **Develop others**: Empower the next generation to lead boldly.
- **Model consistency**: Be the leader your team can count on.
- **Celebrate collective success**: Make team achievements visible.
- **Reflect and adapt**: Continue learning and adjusting with humility.

☑ REAL-WORLD EXAMPLE: MULTIPLYING LEADERSHIP THROUGH MENTORSHIP

In the military, one of the most significant accomplishments a leader can achieve is to influence the next generation. In one of my assignments, I served as an Airman Leadership School Instructor.

The Airman Leadership School was responsible for conducting a five-week professional military education course that taught junior enlisted members leadership theory, emotional intelligence, supervisory communication, and other critical concepts needed to be an effective Non-Commissioned Officer.

Throughout the program, I watched many talented and promising new leaders grow, **shifting from "I" to "we"** as they stepped into supervisory roles. As instructors, we poured our hearts into those five weeks, not just teaching theory, but sharing real-world stories and principles that would serve them long after they left the classroom.

Over the past decade, I've been lucky enough to have met many of my former students from this program. They not only remember me but are eager to share stories of how they are still using the same leadership concepts we studied together. Some of them had become instructors themselves, passing the torch to others.

These experiences helped me see that legacy isn't just about what you teach or accomplish, it's about what gets carried forward long after you're gone.

📃 HISTORICAL EXAMPLE: BOOKER T. WASHINGTON AND THE POWER OF GENERATIONAL INFLUENCE

Booker T. Washington was born into slavery and later became one of the most influential Black educators and leaders of the late 19th and early 20th centuries.

Washington understood the enduring power of leadership legacy. As the founder of Tuskegee Institute, he taught skills while also building leaders.

Washington believed that education, discipline, and self-reliance were essential tools for uplifting entire communities.

He knew that the accurate measure of his work wouldn't be seen in his lifetime; rather, it would be seen in the lives of those his students went on to influence.

One of Washington's most impactful legacies was the chain of leadership he sparked by investing in others.

His mentorship gave rise to future thinkers, educators, and change-makers, such as George Washington Carver, whose own legacy transformed agriculture, science, and sustainability in America.

Washington's story reminds us that legacy isn't about position, it's about multiplication. Washington invested in leaders who would go on to lead others.

🔗 CONNECTION ACROSS TIME: LEGACY THROUGH MULTIPLICATION

Just like Booker T. Washington, modern leaders have the power to leave behind something far greater than a completed checklist or a decorated resume. Legacy is built in the intentional, daily choices to coach others, model integrity, and share what truly matters.

Whether you're training new employees, mentoring a peer, or teaching a classroom of future leaders, **every interaction becomes an opportunity to multiply your influence.**

Legacy happens when your leadership becomes someone else's launchpad. When we lead out loud, boldly, consistently, and with compassion, we shape the present and echo into the future.

🔧 TOOLS TO LEAD YOUR LEGACY

- **Create a leadership philosophy**: Write down the principles that define how you lead.
- **Document key processes**: Make it easy for others to step into critical roles.
- **Invest in mentorship**: Intentionally develop and guide future leaders.
- **Encourage feedback loops**: Promote a culture of continuous learning and improvement.
- **Practice gratitude**: Regularly recognize those who contribute to your mission.

CHAPTER REFLECTION: LEADING WITH LEGACY

Some think that legacy is just about being remembered, but it's actually much more. It is about making a lasting difference. **Every decision, every word, every action has the potential to ripple far beyond your time in a role.**

Reflection Questions:

- What kind of leader do I want to be remembered as?
- How am I preparing others to succeed after me?
- What can I do today to strengthen my leadership footprint?

💡 LEADERSHIP TOOL: LEGACY LEADERSHIP PLANNER

Use this planner to be intentional about the leadership legacy you're building every day.

- ☑ My leadership philosophy: _____
- ☑ Future leaders I'm mentoring: _____
- ☑ Processes I need to document: _____
- ☑ Ways I reinforce culture daily: _____
- ☑ My next step to build legacy: _____

🧩 CONNECTION TO THE L.E.A.D. MODEL

Legacy is the culmination of everything you've practiced:

- **Listening** with empathy
- **Empowering** others with trust
- **Adapting** through change
- **Deciding** with integrity and vision

To *lead out loud* is to leave behind a legacy that continues to grow, even after your voice has moved on.

🌳 BONUS LEADERSHIP NUGGET #11: PLANT OAKS, NOT STATUES

Don't just work to be admired. Work to be multiplied.

MYTH: The best leaders carve their legacy in stone, chasing applause, collecting trophies, and making sure their name echoes long after they're gone.

TRUTH: You want to know what lasts? Not statues, not plaques, not your name in some speech. The real legacy, the kind you feel in your bones, grows roots, not rust. Statues just stand there, looking impressive for a while, until they start to crack or fade. Oaks? They keep going. They spread. They build forests.

I've watched plenty of leaders wear themselves out, chasing the spotlight for a highlight reel. I fell into that trap, too, thinking the best measure of a life was some shiny plaque or my name on a wall. Here's the punch to the gut no one warns you about: Admiration fades fast. Stone weathers. Statues are for people passing through.

The ones who make a real dent are never the folks fussing over their monument; they're the ones who spend less time being admired and a whole lot more time building up the people around them.

Here's the real test: You don't leave a mark by being the hero in your own story. **You leave a legacy by making other people the heroes in their own lives.**

Every time you lift someone, back them in a hard moment, or **put their name out front instead of your own, you're planting something** that'll last way longer than any banner with your face on it.

Statues reflect who you were. Oaks show what you gave away. One stops at your story; the other keeps growing because you did.

If you really want to measure your leadership, look past the crowd that claps at your send-off. Ask yourself: Who's standing taller because you had their back? Your legacy isn't about the crowd you gather, it's about the forest you plant.

So, plant wisely. Don't just work to be admired, work to be multiplied, plant oaks, not statues.

The world doesn't need more monuments. It needs more forests and leaders bold enough to get their hands in the dirt and help something else grow.

🌱 Leadership Nugget Reflection Prompts: Plant Oaks, Not Statues

These prompts help you examine whether you're leading for admiration or multiplication. Statues leave an impression. Oaks leave a legacy.

Reflection Prompts

1. Where am I chasing recognition instead of replication?

2. What daily habits or choices are planting seeds in others?

3. Who have I mentored that's now mentoring someone else?

4. If I left today, what part of my leadership would still grow?

5. Do I celebrate personal wins, or shared growth?

6. What am I building that doesn't need my name on it to thrive?

⊛ Practice It Out Loud: Build What Outgrows You.

Legacy is built in moments, not monuments. Here's how to put it into action.

✳ *Four-Step Guide to Practicing It Out Loud:*

1. **Identify a Seed Worth Planting**

   What leadership value, habit, or mindset do you want others to carry forward?
   ☞ *"This week, I want to model ___, so it multiplies."*

2. **Name Your Multipliers**

   Who on your team is ready to be poured into?
   ☞ *"Who can I intentionally invest in this week?"*

3. **Share the Story, Not Just the Skill**

   Oaks grow roots through connection. Don't just delegate, share the why behind the what.
   ☞ *"How can I tell the story behind this leadership lesson?"*

4. **Celebrate Quiet Impact**

   Leadership legacy isn't about being seen, it's about being repeated.
   ☞ *"Who quietly made a ripple this week that deserves recognition?"*

📓 REFLECTION JOURNAL – MEASURING YOUR LEADERSHIP ECHO

Turn today's margin into tomorrow's momentum

Use this space to track how your leadership is multiplying. What did you pass on today that could grow tomorrow?

Date	Person or Team	What You Planted	What Multiplied or Grew

CONCLUSION

CLOSING SUMMARY: LEADING OUT LOUD, EVERY DAY

Leadership isn't huge personalities, grand speeches, or formal titles.

Leadership happens every day, in fleeting moments, when you listen with presence, speak with purpose, and lead with clarity.

The L.E.A.D. Model is more than a framework; it's a way of showing up in the world:

- ☑ **Listen with intent**: Begin by listening to others before sharing your thoughts.
- ☑ **Empower through communication**: Use your voice to elevate, not control.
- ☑ **Adapt and overcome**: Communicate clearly in chaos and pivot with grace.
- ☑ **Decide and deliver**: Lead with conviction and clarity in moments that matter.

Leadership is not just what you say, but what you *signal* every day. Your tone, timing, and trustworthiness all convey a powerful message. To *lead out loud* is to lead with authenticity, vision, and human connection.

Whether you're briefing a commander, mentoring a teammate, or guiding a community, your voice is your leadership.

Own it. Sharpen it. Speak it with purpose, because leadership isn't just about who follows you, it's about what you leave behind.

🌲 FINAL BONUS LEADERSHIP NUGGET: DON'T JUST LEAD, RESOUND

💧 **MYTH:** Leadership is all about leaving everyone breathless, owning the spotlight, being the loudest in the room, and burning through the finish line with nothing left in the tank. "Go out in a blaze," they say. "Make them miss you."

TRUTH: Here's what experience actually teaches: Anyone can make a scene, but not many can make a difference that sticks around. **Real leaders aren't measured by applause; they're measured by what lasts after the crowd goes home and your email drops from everyone's inbox.** You don't build legacy by running yourself into the ground; you do it by building something (and someone) that outlasts you.

I used to believe the myth, and I committed myself repeatedly to validating that belief. I thought hustling harder, being everywhere at once, and leaving completely spent was noble. I'd prided myself on being the first boot (person) that hit the ground (arrive) and the last boot to go, thinking that effort coupled with exhaustion was the proof of leadership. Turns out, all I proved was that I could burn out with the best of them. Do you want to know how that affected my team? They were left squinting in the smoke, wondering how to keep going now that I was gone.

The thing about being loud only is that it doesn't echo for long. What stays with people isn't your volume or your all-nighters. What sticks with people is whether your example, your trust, your actual care for their growth gave them the guts and the clarity to keep climbing after you left the room.

I've seen and been the leaders who burn themselves out for the win, leaving nothing but charred ground. I've also seen the quiet ones, the ones who pass the torch while there's still plenty of light and fuel to give, turn teams into movements, and the next generation into torchbearers. **So, here's what I ask myself now, and I beg you to ask it too:**

Are you leaving anything behind that someone else can build on, or are you just burning bright and fast for the sake of it? Have you slowed down long enough to show someone else the rope, the reasons or the "why" behind your fire? Do your people feel steady, not just inspired? Did you prep your team to keep lighting the way, even when your name stops trending in their heads?

Noise fades. Impact sticks.

Don't just aim for a dramatic exit, aim for a legacy that keeps lighting fires long after you're gone.

Make sure you're not just remembered. Make sure what you built is still moving.

Finish whole, not hollow. Don't just light the moment, ignite the movement. That's leadership that echoes long after the lights go down.

🎺 Leadership Nugget Reflection Prompts: Don't Just Lead, Resound

These prompts help you explore the lasting sound of your leadership, what echoes, what fades, and what matters most.

Reflection Prompts

1. What's the message my leadership sends, even when I'm silent?

2. Do people repeat my ideas because they're memorable, or just convenient?

3. When was the last time I led in a way that changed someone's life in the long term, not just in the short term?

4. What am I doing now to shape the legacy of my voice?

5. If my leadership were to be echoed by someone else, what would it sound like?

6. Have I been chasing attention or building alignment?

7. What is one action I can take this week to speak with more clarity and conviction?

💡 *Your impact isn't measured by how often you speak, but by how deeply your words and actions live on.*

Practice It Out Loud: Build the Echo

You don't need a louder voice, just one that *lasts longer*. These intentional moves help you align your leadership with clarity, conviction, and echo-worthy impact.

✳ *Four-Step Guide to Practicing It Out Loud:*

1. **Define Your Leadership Echo**

    What's the one thing you want people to remember when you're no longer in the room?
    ☞ *Write it. Say it. Lead it.*

2. **Anchor Your Actions to Your Message.**

    Does your calendar reflect your core values?
    ☞ *One aligned action is more powerful than ten empty messages.*

3. **Reinforce, Don't Just Repeat**

    Legacy builds through consistency.
    ☞ *What is one message your team needs to hear again, but with deeper conviction?*

4. **Choose Moments That Carry**

    Not every moment needs a speech.
    ☞ *Pick the moments that matter and deliver them with purpose, so they echo longer than they last.*

📘 REFLECTION JOURNAL – ECHOING IMPACT

Turn your final words into lasting waves

Leadership doesn't stop at the sound of your voice, it lives on in the conversations it inspires, the courage it ignites, and the choices it shapes. Use this space to capture the ripple effect of your leadership in motion.

Where did your leadership echo today?
What did others carry forward without you prompting them?
What moment proved your voice had outlived your presence?

Date	Moment of Impact	What Was Carried Forward	What Echoed Back

💬 A PERSONAL NOTE FROM ME TO YOU

If you're here at the final line, you've done more than read, you've answered the call. That says everything and thank you.

This book wasn't written in safety or silence. It was hammered out in the heat of tension, between comfort and courage, between waiting for permission and daring to act.

I didn't write it for those collecting accolades.

I wrote it for the ones who lead on quiet days, the unseen, the underestimated and the uncelebrated. The ones who show up tired, questioned, uncertain...and still stand tall.

Leadership isn't reserved for the flawless. It's claimed daily by those bold enough to rise anyway, not with perfect plans, but with unshakable purpose

Here's the truth, most won't say out loud:

You don't need a bigger title.

You don't need a brighter spotlight.

You just need conviction, the kind that stands its ground, even when no one's clapping.

You need to stop waiting for the green light.

This is not a handbook. It's a handoff. Not a torch, but a relay. A movement passed from one voice to the next, not to carry alone but to multiply.

So this is your rally point.

Stand up. Speak the truth only you can tell. Don't dim your voice until it's "safe."

Be the proof that legacy isn't what you leave behind someday, it's what you build now, every time you choose courage over silence.

The echo the world needs? It doesn't come from echoing others. It starts with your voice. **Louder. Clearer. Braver.**

This isn't the end of your chapter. It's the spark of a movement. So go, lead loud enough that when the world gets quiet, your voice is still the one that lights the way.

Live it. Speak it. Build it. Legacy isn't given. It's made, and it starts with you.

APPENDIX: TOOLS & TEMPLATES

Appendix: Tools & Templates

This appendix includes all the worksheets, tools, and reflection exercises referenced throughout *L.E.A.D. Out Loud*. These resources are designed to help you apply the principles of the L.E.A.D. Model in practical, actionable ways.

Chapter 1: Listen with Intent

Tool: Listening Prep & Practice Guide

- ✓ Block 15 distraction-free minutes before next 1-on-1
- ✓ Write 2 open-ended questions to ask
- ✓ Practice the 3-second pause
- ✓ Keep a journal of one listening lesson per week

Chapter 2: Empower Through Communication

Tool: Empowerment Conversation Starter Kit

- ✓ "What would you do in my place?"
- ✓ "What strengths do you see in yourself?"
- ✓ "Where do you want to grow and how can I help?"
- ✓ "What's something you've never been asked to lead?"

Chapter 3: Adapt and Overcome

Tool: Crisis Communication Prep Sheet

- ☑ Identify 3 core talking points
- ☑ Draft "What we know / What we're doing / What's next"
- ☑ Select delivery methods (email, call, huddle)
- ☑ Write one confidence-building phrase

Chapter 4: Decide and Deliver

Tool: Decision Clarity Checklist

- ☑ Input gathered from stakeholders?
- ☑ Aligned with mission and values?
- ☑ Clarity in consequences and next steps?

ᴵᴵᴵ RAPID DECISION MATRIX

Use this matrix when under pressure:

IRREVERSIBLE	REVERSIBLE
Pause Briefly, Gather Input, Then Act	Delegate & Decide
Decide & Communicate the "Why"	Gather Buy-In, Then Decide
Decide & Be Present	Decide & Correct as Needed

Chapter 5: The Voice of Influence

Tool: Daily Vocal Prep Checklist

- ☑ 1-minute breathing & grounding
- ☑ 30 seconds of articulation warm-up
- ☑ Power stance or stretch
- ☑ Practice intentional silence

Chapter 6: Mastering Connection Through Storytelling

Tool: Storytelling Framework

- ☑ Relatable character
- ☑ Clear challenge or conflict
- ☑ Turning point
- ☑ Resolution / Lesson
- ☑ Call to action

Chapter 7: Building Clarity Through Message Design

Tool: Message Design Planner

- ☑ One core message
- ☑ Three key points
- ☑ Analogy or example
- ☑ Why it matters
- ☑ Best delivery method

Chapter 8: Developing Connection Through Emotional Intelligence

Tool: Emotional Intelligence Daily Check-In

- ☑ What am I feeling?
- ☑ What are others feeling?
- ☑ Did I pause before responding?
- ☑ Did I express empathy or instruction?

Chapter 9: Inspiring Action Through Vision and Purpose

Tool: Vision & Purpose Canvas

- ☑ Our Vision:
- ☑ Why It Matters:
- ☑ Who It Serves:
- ☑ Success Looks Like:
- ☑ Key Milestones:

Chapter 10: Sustaining Leadership Energy and Resilience

Tool: Energy & Resilience Tracker

- ☑ Sleep hours:
- ☑ What energized me today:
- ☑ Current stress level:

- ☑ What helped me recover:
- ☑ Small win to celebrate:

Chapter 11: Final Reflections and Leading Your Legacy

Tool: Legacy Leadership Planner

- ☑ My leadership philosophy:
- ☑ People I'm mentoring:
- ☑ Processes to document:
- ☑ Culture-building habits:
- ☑ Legacy step I'll take this week:

Use these templates as part of your leadership practice, journaling routine, coaching strategy, or team development process.

You can print, replicate, or adapt them to your context. Stay consistent. Stay connected. *Lead out loud.*

🌳 PLANT OAKS, NOT STATUES

Thank you for showing up, for leaning in, and for choosing to lead out loud, but this mission doesn't stop here.

Leadership isn't about building monuments to be admired. It's about planting roots, deep ones that grow into something far bigger than you.

It's about **planting oaks**, not statues, and this message? It's meant to take root and spread.

🌱 How You Can Help Grow the Mission:

1. 📝 **Leave a Quick Review**

   It doesn't have to be fancy. Just honest.
   Your words might be the spark someone else needs to unlock their voice.

2. 📱 **Scan the QR code or go to:**

   https://bit.ly/leadoutloud-klg

3. 🎁Download the Free L.E.A.D. Starter Kit

These are the same tools I use to coach mission-driven leaders worldwide. Now they're yours.

💻 *Get yours at:*
knightleadershipgroups.com

4. 📲 Speak It Forward

Post your favorite quote. Share a reflection. Tag a teammate. Let the echo of your growth reach someone else.

Use: **#LEADOutLoud**
Tag: **@LeadwithAntawn**

5. 📚 Pass It On

Know someone hungry for clarity or purpose?
Gift them this book.
Give them their moment. *Because leadership isn't for the spotlight, it's for the ripple effect.*

⚡ Final Word

L.E.A.D. Out Loud wasn't written to be a conclusion.
It was planted to become a movement, and now, you're part of it.

So, keep leading with courage.

Keep speaking with clarity.

Keep planting the kind of leadership that outlasts you.

With belief in your voice,
~ Antawn Knight
Be Clear. Be Heard. Be Unstoppable.

📢 LET'S KEEP THE MOVEMENT GOING

If you've made it this far, **thank you**.

You didn't just read this book. You showed up. You leaned in. You chose to grow, and that means everything.

But this message? It's bigger than these pages.
It's a movement.

I'd love for you to help me carry it forward, louder, clearer, and further than ever.

Here's How You Can Help Amplify the Mission:

1. 📝 **Leave a Quick Review**

   It doesn't have to be fancy. Just honest.
   Your words might be the spark someone else needs to unlock their voice.

   📱 *Scan the QR code or go to:*

   https://bit.ly/leadoutloud-klg

2. 🎁 **Download Your Free L.E.A.D. Starter Kit & Join L.E.A.D. Academy**

   These are the same tools I use to coach leaders around the world, ready for you to apply right now.

   💻 *Get yours at:*
   [KnightLeadershipGroups.com]

3. 🗂 **Share Your Voice Online**

   Post your favorite quote. Tag a friend. Highlight your "aha" moment.
   Show others what it looks like to lead out loud.

Use: **#LEADOutLoud**
Tag: **@LeadWithAntawn**

4. 📚 **Pass It Forward**

    Know someone searching for clarity or purpose?
    Gift them this book. Give them their moment.
    Leadership isn't about hoarding wisdom; it's about
    multiplying it.

💬 Final Thought

L.E.A.D. Out Loud was never meant to be the last word, it's just the
beginning.
Your part of something bigger now. A movement of leaders who
show up with courage, speak with clarity, and leave legacy in
their wake.

Let's keep that echo going.

With respect and purpose,
~ Antawn Knight
Be Clear. Be Heard. Be Unstoppable.

📚 RECOMMENDED READING & INFLUENTIAL WORKS

The following authors and books significantly influenced the
leadership principles explored in *L.E.A.D. Out Loud*. While not all
are directly quoted, their frameworks, stories, and philosophies
shaped many of the ideas throughout this book:

- **Blanchard, Ken & Johnson, Spencer.** *The One Minute Manager.*
- **Brown, Brené.** *Dare to Lead.*
- **Carnegie, Dale.** *How to Win Friends and Influence People.*
- **Covey, Stephen R.** *The 7 Habits of Highly Effective People.*
- **Duckworth, Angela.** *Grit.*
- **Gladwell, Malcolm.** *Blink.*
- **Goleman, Daniel.** *Emotional Intelligence.*
- **Grenny, Joseph, et al.** *Crucial Conversations.*
- **Heath, Chip & Heath, Dan.** *Made to Stick.*
- **Maxwell, John C.** *The 5 Levels of Leadership.*
- **Sinek, Simon.** *Start with Why.*
- **Willink, Jocko & Babin, Leif.** *Extreme Ownership.*
- **Zenger, Jack & Folkman, Joseph.** *The Extraordinary Leader.*

REFERENCES

Below is a curated list of specific works, quotations, and research cited or foundational to the book's insights on communication, leadership, resilience, and clarity:

BOOKS & THOUGHT LEADERSHIP

Bennis, Warren. *On Becoming a Leader.* Basic Books, 1989.

- Carnegie, Dale. *How to Win Friends and Influence People.* Simon & Schuster, 1936.

- Covey, Stephen R. *The 7 Habits of Highly Effective People.* Free Press, 1989.

- Goleman, Daniel. *Emotional Intelligence: Why It Can Matter More Than IQ.* Bantam, 1995.

- Heath, Chip & Heath, Dan. *Made to Stick: Why Some Ideas Survive and Others Die.* Random House, 2007.

- Maxwell, John C. *The 5 Levels of Leadership: Proven Steps to Maximize Your Potential.* Center Street, 2011.

- Patterson, Kerry, et al. *Crucial Conversations: Tools for Talking When Stakes Are High.* McGraw-Hill, 2002.

- Sinek, Simon. *Start with Why: How Great Leaders Inspire Everyone to Take Action.* Portfolio, 2009.

QUOTATIONS & INFLUENCES

- Einstein, Albert. Quotation on clarity and simplicity.
- Holloway, Mary. Quotation on resilience and personal strength.
- Humes, James. Quotation on communication and leadership.
- Reagan, Ronald. Quotation on leadership and empowering others.
- Roosevelt, Theodore. Quotation on decision-making urgency.

MILITARY & LEADERSHIP DOCTRINE

- Department of Defense Financial Management Regulations
- ICASS (International Cooperative Administrative Support Services) Governance Guidelines
- Professional Military Education (PME) Curriculum Standards
- U.S. Air Force Leadership Principles

COMMUNICATION & PSYCHOLOGY RESEARCH

- Atkinson, Clifford. *Beyond Bullet Points.* Research cited for the Three-Point Message Rule and audience retention.

- Edmondson, Amy. Harvard Business School: Psychological Safety in Teams

- Mehrabian, Albert. *Silent Messages.* Research on verbal vs. nonverbal communication impact.

ABOUT THE AUTHOR

 **Antawn Knight** is a dynamic leadership strategist, senior military leader, and author of *L.E.A.D. Out Loud: Be Clear. Be Heard. Be Unstoppable.* With over 15 years of experience leading global teams, managing multi-million-dollar operations, and developing future leaders, Antawn has become a trusted voice in mission-driven leadership and communication.

A Senior Non-Commissioned Officer in the United States Air Force, he has served across four continents and led initiatives that bridge strategic planning with human-centered leadership. From mentoring rising professionals to managing inter-agency diplomacy at the U.S. Embassy in Australia, Antawn's leadership is grounded in service, clarity, and connection.

His L.E.A.D. Model: **Listen with Intent, Empower Through Communication, Adapt and Overcome, Decide and Deliver,** has helped teams thrive under pressure and emerge with purpose.

Antawn speaks, writes, and coaches on transformational leadership, emotional intelligence, and the power of voice in shaping culture. When he's not leading teams or training the next generation of leaders, you can find him exploring nature, creating with his family, or championing meaningful conversations that move people and organizations forward.

https://www.knightleadershipgroups.com/
amazon.com/author/antawnknight

www.ingramcontent.com/pod-product-compliance
Lightning Source LLC
Chambersburg PA
CBHW060153130626
46556CB00006B/2624